Contents

W9-BXX-440

Acknowledgments

Together we would like to thank our past and present students for asking us the questions that created the need for this book. We would also like to thank our colleagues, as well as the many industry professionals, casting directors, agents, actors, and teachers who helped in the guidance of this book.

Special thanks to Mari Lyn Henry for agreeing to meet with us on such a cold and rainy day, and for her advice and generous assistance in getting this project to Back Stage Books.

Thanks to Michèle LaRue, our editor, who took this book to extraordinary levels by challenging us through her expertise, honesty, humor, and patience to go back (again and again) and find the right words.

Thanks to Mark Glubke, Senior Editor at Back Stage Books, for his full support and belief in this book, and for trusting us with the project.

Thanks to Rita Rosenkranz, our agent, for navigating us through the channels, and to Chad Thompson for his brilliant and hilarious illustrations.

Darren R. Cohen and Michael Perilstein

I would like to thank my close friends, family, and students for their constant support, and for pushing me to write this book. Thank you Bob Cline, Rich Cole Casting, Pat McCorkle Casting, Liz Ortiz-Mackes at Casting Solutions, Jay Binder Casting, Lesley Collis at Mattel Casting, Laura Richin Casting, Liz Lewis Casting Partners, Mark Simon Casting, Norman Meranus Casting, Stephanie Klapper Casting, Alan Filderman Casting, Cindi Rush Casting, Margaret Emory, John Simpkins, William Westbrooks, William Schill, Josh Pultz, Jeffrey Dunn, Bill Cox, David Caldwell, James Stenborg, David and Jan Martin, Michael Sartor, Elaine Petricoff, my accountant, Leanne Greenberg, and Mark Sendroff for his advice.

Special thanks to my sister Lauren Cohen, for encouraging me to keep writing.

Darren R. Cohen

Much thanks and appreciation go to the faculty of the University of Virginia Drama Department, particularly Kate Burke, Bob Chapel, Betsy Tucker, and Richard Warner. Thanks also to Colleen Kelly at the University of San Diego. Many of the ideas and exercises found in this book were directly influenced by their work as educators and actors, and to them I am most grateful.

Thanks to Scott Eck of the Laughingstock Company, for showing me there should always be "something on the line," and that Tomato is funny, but Asparagus is funnier. Thanks, too, to Walleyed Productions, for their support, and to William Mastrosimone for his generosity. Thanks also to the American Musical and Dramatic Academy, and to the faculty who teach there. I would be hard pressed to find a more professional group of dedicated, talented teachers.

I would also like to thank my parents and family for their unyielding encouragement and support. To whatever ideas I brought up to them they never said, "Why?"; instead they always said, "Why not?"

In addition, I would especially like to thank Robbie for having to endure my ongoing monologues throughout the process of writing this book. I'm sure it all seemed endless. Her constant input and advice usually ended with her saying: "Stop talking about it and start writing it."

And to Spalding Gray, who continues to inspire. Thank You.

Michael Perilstein

Foreword

There are some actors, maybe one-tenth of one percent of all the actors in the theater, who can convince everyone of their talent and brilliance just by walking into a room. It doesn't matter what they say, whether they're well prepared, what they're wearing, whether they've slept in the last week, if one of their eyeballs is leaking pus all over the room; they're still perfect and anyone can see it. This book is not for them.

There are some actors, maybe a larger percentage than the previous group, who will never work professionally unless they actually buy a Broadway theater. They could spend every day of the rest of their lives taking lessons, studying with coaches, eating right, working out, learning the perfect monologue, buying the best dance shoes; it doesn't matter—somehow they communicate "cataclysm" simply by waking up in the morning. This book is not for them.

Everyone else who auditions for the theater—this book is for you. I have sat in front of thousands of actors over the last fifteen years, watching them all with the hope that they'll be the right person to breathe life into my character, and every one of those thousands of people could have benefited from at least one of the succinctly written and well-considered pieces of advice that Darren and Michael offer in these pages. Some of those auditioners actually could have benefited from every single piece of advice in these pages.

No one in the theater knows everything, and there are in fact times when it seems that no one in the theater knows anything at all, but Darren and Michael have prepared a very valuable guide to the torturous process of auditioning. I see so many talented and wonderful actors who loathe auditioning so much that they freeze up or project their bile every time they have to go in. Lots of other actors are just confused and disoriented by having to "show their stuff" on command in less-than-perfect settings. And plenty of other actors walk out of every audition feeling like they could have, should have, would have done better if only, if only, if only. Here's something you might not know: we on the other side of the table don't love auditions much either, and as soon as someone figures out a better way to cast a show, we'll be the first ones to sign up. Until then, when you as an actor are called upon to expose yourself and your art for a brief instant in the hope that you'll be considered "right" for the job, I think you can rely on *The Complete Professional Audition* to support you through that process. To risk a cliché, Break a leg!

Jason Robert Brown
Los Angeles, California
March 2005

Preface

If you browse through the Performing Arts section of a bookstore, you are likely to find many books that focus on auditioning for the theater. So, why write this one? Do performers really need another "how-to" book?

When researching the different kinds of books on the subject, I found dozens of volumes on musical theater and on nonmusical theater. What was missing was a book that combined both—in great detail.

As a musical director and vocal coach, I have learned that singers hesitate to audition for plays, either because they are afraid to or because they simply don't know how. Conversely, I have also met many nonmusical theater actors who sing well, but are afraid to audition with a song because they don't know how to prepare.

The Complete Professional Audition: A Commonsense Guide to Auditioning for Musicals and Plays addresses the fears and concerns of both kinds of performers, by explaining in detail the similarities and differences between musical and nonmusical auditions. When you have finished reading this book, you will have a thorough understanding of the audition process, from finding material to signing a contract.

Part One focuses on everything you need to know about preparing for your musical theater audition. In Part Two, I have asked monologue expert Michael Perilstein to discuss in detail how to find and prepare monologues for your nonmusical (and musical) auditions. Part Three offers practical information that applies to both types of auditions and lifestyles—such as putting together a résumé and finding an agent. This section also explores many networking options and tactics, and suggests various ways to support yourself in the business. Because Michael and I are based in New York City, we've referred to many resources there. But since we've also worked in the outer regions and on the road, we know that with a little imagination and resourcefulness, you'll find similar opportunities in whatever metropolis you choose to live, audition, and take center stage.

—*Darren R. Cohen*

Introduction

So many actors have been led to believe that their God-given talent alone will bring them success. We see so many extraordinarily talented actors enter the business of acting and disappear within a few short years because of professional disappointment. This is sad because if these people were educated on how to become professional actors, as opposed to only being educated on how to act, they would probably have the careers they had hoped for originally.

In acting, as in any business, many factors play an important part as you work to achieve your goals. There are no direct paths leading to success, and almost everyone you talk to will have taken a different journey to get to where he or she is. In fact, one actor's successful approach can be another's big mistake. Yet there is a method for getting through the madness: simple common sense.

As coaches and educators, as a musical director, and as an actor in New York City, we are often asked the same questions, over and over: How do I get started? How do I find an agent? What should I wear to an audition? Should I take this job? What exactly is a casting director? Do I need to send a thank-you note? That's just to name a few.

With this book we intend to clear up many of the myths, questions, and contradictions about working in the theater—and to provide insight into the audition process. Our suggested dos and don'ts reflect what the "business" considers to be industry standard. These are not cut-and-dried *rules*: they may waver under specific circumstances or be affected by your own unique qualities as an actor and as an individual. Some are based on instinct; some are embedded in tradition. Sorting them out calls for . . . common sense.

To consider, to have, and to enjoy a career in the theater, actors must process and juggle a wealth of important information. There are so many opportunities and pitfalls and tools and techniques that we wish we had known about when we started. This book is our way of sharing them with you. Consider *The Complete Professional Audition: A Commonsense Guide to Auditioning for Musicals and Plays* to be a quick reference course on *everything you need to know about getting the job and keeping your career going.* Read it, use it—and get working!

—*Darren R. Cohen and Michael Perilstein*

PART ONE
Musical Theater Auditions

CHAPTER 1

Finding and Choosing the Right Song for Your Audition

To audition for a musical, you need to prepare appropriate songs that will demonstrate both your vocal and acting skills. In looking for the right songs, many factors should be taken into consideration, such as your voice, age, and physical type, the style of the show you are auditioning for, and your personal taste. Not every song is right for every person.

In searching for audition material, please understand that there is no such thing as the "perfect" song! It simply does not exist. The criterion for the "perfect" song is first and foremost one that you like. If you don't enjoy singing it, don't use it. If you can't connect to the lyrics dramatically and emotionally, don't use it.

However, I do urge you to investigate material that doesn't interest you right away, because certain songs may grow on you the more you study them. (Just as your friends do.)

VOCAL REQUIREMENTS

When choosing a song, you want to show the strongest and most secure parts of your vocal range. Remember that the high notes you reach while vocalizing with your voice teacher may not be notes that you sing comfortably in a song. The song may need to be transposed to a better key for you if you want to use it at an audition.

AGE APPROPRIATENESS

When choosing material, it is very important to consider the age that you project. If you are twenty-seven years old but still look twenty-one, you need to find material that matches your look. You have to see yourself as a product that you are trying to market. Having unusual maturity and life experience doesn't matter too much if you look young. Those auditioning you can only use what they see on the outside. For example, a teenage girl who *looks* between the ages of sixteen and twenty-one can easily use the song "Much More" from *The Fantasticks* because the role of Luisa is written for a young, naïve girl. When this hypothetical actress begins to look older, her performance as Luisa may be hard to believe. On the other hand, a twenty-five-year-old actress who looks eighteen can effectively use the song.

DRAMATIC TONE

Find material that is positive in nature rather than offensive and cynical. Keep away from hate songs, suicide songs, sexual-orientation songs, and parodies, because you never know whom you may insult (or frighten).

The people for whom you're auditioning are called the "auditors," or the audition panel. (For a list of who those people might be, see "Who Is Usually Sitting Behind the Audition Table?," Chapter 6, page 40). They assume that you want to show them a part of your personality through the material you have selected for your audition. That's another good reason to stay away from hate songs. It's also a very good reason to stay away from songs that you hate to sing. The worst thing you can do is to audition with a particular song simply because your coach or teacher told you to do so. You need to take part in this decision. It's like shopping for your own clothes—you are the one who has to wear the outfit that you've bought, and you want to be comfortable in it.

LENGTH

Very often at an audition you'll be instructed to sing only sixteen bars of a song. (See Chapter 3, "Defining Sixteen Bars," beginning on page 27). I urge you to stay away from narrative story songs, as, dramatically speaking, they are very difficult to cut down to sixteen bars. Examples of these would be "Meadowlark" from *The Baker's Wife*, or "The Saga of Jenny" from *Lady in the Dark*. It is virtually impossible to cut down fifteen pages of a story effectively to sixteen bars, and more like telling the punch line of a joke without the setup.

Composers who often write story songs are Kurt Weill, Stephen Sondheim, Stephen Schwartz, Jason Robert Brown, Richard Maltby Jr., and David Shire. Of course, not *all* of their compositions are story songs.

Even if you are asked to sing a full song, there are plenty of songs that will accomplish what you need to do without boring the panel with a story song that has eight verses of the same repeating music.

REPETITION

Avoid songs with repetitious melody lines. What a waste of your time it is to attempt to demonstrate your range by only using three or four different notes in your sixteen-bar cut! Examples of this kind of repetition are "The Man I Love" from *Lady Be Good* by George and Ira Gershwin (see pages 5–7) and "Just in Time" from *Bells Are Ringing* by Jule Styne, Betty Comden, and Adolf Green.

SIGNATURE SONGS

Think twice about choosing songs that are too connected to specific star performers.

The Man I Love

The Man I Love (continued)

"People," for example, is associated with Barbra Streisand, and "Cabaret" with Liza Minelli. Not only are these kinds of songs overdone, but sometimes the auditors can't help comparing you to the performer they have always associated with that song.

WHAT IF THE AUTHORS ARE PRESENT?

If the composer and/or lyricist will be present at the audition, it is usually suggested that you not sing one of their songs, initially. (Unless, of course, this has been requested in the casting notice.) You don't want the authors to focus on *their* material; the focus should be on *you*. The original performer and/or cast recording still lingers in their ears, so for you to top these artists is nearly impossible. If you don't perform the authors' song to their liking, they'll have trouble seeing past that—and you'll have lost your potential callback.

I encourage you to find material that is stylistically similar to the show and that will help the panel see you in the role you have been submitted for or are interested in. If you are strongly being considered for a role (as opposed to the chorus), then you will probably be asked to learn one of the songs from the actual show being produced. When I was casting a revival of *Dear World*, many people auditioned with songs from that show. Composer-lyricist Jerry Herman was at the auditions and very graciously told each of them he would rather hear something else first, so he could look at them objectively. He felt that his ear was too critical of and subjective to performances of his own material. He needed to focus on the singers' talents, not on how well they presented his songs. If they were invited to the callbacks, then material from the show would be requested.

STYLE OF THE SHOW

Make sure you have carefully read the casting notice. Remember that ninety percent of the time, the style of music that the panel needs to hear at an audition is spelled out for you in the casting notice.

Find out ahead of time as much as possible about the creative team and its work. What else have the authors written? Does their writing always encompass one certain style? Is this particular show set in a specific period of history? Is the show based on an ethnic theme? Once you have identified the specifics, look at the material you have. Which is the most appropriate for this audition? Choosing a song from *Les Misérables* to use at an audition for *Anything Goes* shows the panel that you have no understanding of style, and/or that you didn't bother to do any research.

Les Misérables was written in the late 1980s. Its music adds a "pop" flair to the dramatic classic style of Rodgers and Hammerstein, and its book deals with tragedies of the French Revolution. *Anything Goes* was written in the 1930s. Its music is bouncy, reflecting the Roaring Twenties and incorporating such dances as the Charleston; there's a light, playful quality to the show.

In looking for a song that fits the style of *Les Misérables*, I would suggest something from *Jekyll & Hyde*, *The Scarlet Pimpernel*, *The Secret Garden*, *Martin Guerre*, *Ragtime*, or *Titanic*; for *Anything Goes*, I would consider a song from *The Boyfriend*, *Crazy for You*, *42nd Street*, *Babes in Arms*, or *No, No, Nanette*.

If you do your research, and follow through on it, the audition panel will greatly appreciate your effort and sense of responsibility. More importantly, these casting people will get a sense of your ability to perform in the appropriate style.

ASKING TOO MUCH OF THE PIANIST

Be wary of songs that have difficult piano accompaniments. You can't expect an audition pianist to sight-read music that is very complicated to play. Some composers who write a lot of material with busy and difficult piano parts are Stephen Sondheim, Leonard Bernstein, Kurt Weill, David Shire, and Jason Robert Brown. (I am not saying that *all* of their material falls into this category.)

Also, think twice about using sloppy handwritten scores that are very hard to read, especially if you're considering an obscure score that the pianist has probably never seen before. Have a second choice ready to go if necessary.

ARRANGEMENTS

It is wise to stay away from fancy nightclub and clever cabaret musical arrangements. They tend to distract from and sometimes even upstage your work. You are the one auditioning, not your musical arrangements. One exception may be an audition for a musical revue in which the musical arrangements are not so straightforward. Such revues include *Perfectly Frank* (the music of Frank Loesser), *A Grand Night for Singing* (the music of Richard Rodgers), and *Side by Side by Sondheim* (the music of Stephen Sondheim).

Once a song is taken out of the context of its show, there are practically no limits to how an arranger and singer can embellish and interpret it to put their stamp on it. For instance, in the mid-1980s, Barbra Streisand released *The Broadway Album*, containing classic musical theater songs. Among these are "Some Enchanted Evening" from *South Pacific*. In the show this song is sung by a man in his 40s or 50s and is intended to be performed almost like an aria from an opera, without any vocal riffs and ad libs. Streisand obviously took the song out of the 1940s and put her interpretation on it. The harmonic structure was altered and a real pop approach was taken with the musical phrasings. If you were auditioning for a production of *South Pacific*, and used the arrangement printed in *The Broadway Album*, you would not be honoring the original composition in the way the casting people at the audition need to hear it.

FINDERS, KEEPERS

If you find a great song that works for you, don't be quick to give it out to friends, especially if it is hard to find. You can use the same song for years if it still works well for you. Only consider changing your material if you feel that too many people in the industry have heard you use it for too many years, if you simply cannot keep it fresh anymore, or if you have aged beyond it.

FIND PARALLEL SONGS

It is unwise to present a song from the show you are auditioning for unless that song has been specifically requested. Most directors go into an audition with a clear vision of a character. If your rehearsed vision differs from theirs, it can be very difficult for them to see beyond your choices. They may also feel that redirecting you in a short rehearsal period would take too long.

It is very common for a theater to suggest that you sing a song that the composer for this show has written. I think this request can be misleading because composers don't necessarily write in the same style for *every* show. If your local theater were holding auditions for Stephen Sondheim's *Sweeney Todd*, music from *Into the Woods* and *A Little Night Music* would not be very appropriate, due to the vast differences in styles.

For example, when I was conducting a production of *A Little Night Music*, the director and I were seeing young guys for the role of Henrik. The character is an odd, outcast, hermit-like young man harboring a lot of pent-up frustration, and the performer must have a strong tenor vocal range. Most of the actors reading the breakdown immediately thought "Sondheim" and "tenor." So naturally, most of them brought in "Giants in the Sky" from *Into the Woods* and "Love, I Hear" from *A Funny Thing Happened on the Way to the Forum*. Although these songs were written for tenors, neither of the characters who sings them possesses any of Henrik's personality traits. The performers who auditioned with these songs were not helping us to consider them for the role.

Clear examples of parallel songs are "America" from *West Side Story* and "Something Better Than This" from *Sweet Charity*. These have a very similar feel, musically and rhythmically, and yet they are written by two different writers.

Listed below are more examples of songs that parallel each other dramatically and lyrically, though not necessarily in musical style. Many of the examples used are very familiar songs. As always, I encourage you to find songs that aren't so overdone.

THE "WANT" SONG

Show Title	Song Title
Cinderella	"In My Own Little Corner"
The Fantasticks	"Much More"

Hallelujah, Baby!	"My Own Morning"
The King and I	"I Have Dreamed"
Les Misérables	"Castle on a Cloud"
Little Shop of Horrors	"Somewhere That's Green
Newsies	"Santa Fe"
110 in the Shade	"Simple Little Things"
The Secret Garden	"The Girl I Mean to Be"
Smile	"Disneyland"
West Side Story	"Somewhere"
The Wizard of Oz	"Over the Rainbow"

HOPEFUL ROMANTIC

Show Title	Song Title
Brigadoon	"Waiting for My Dearie"
Camelot	"Simple Joys of Maidenhood"
Cinderella	"Some Day My Prince Will Come"
Crazy for You	"Someone to Watch Over Me"
I Can Get It for You Wholesale	"Who Knows?"
Jumbo	"My Romance"
Lady in the Dark	"My Ship"
Most Happy Fella	"Somebody, Somewhere"
Music Man	"Goodnight My Someone"
The Will Rogers Follies	"My Unknown Someone"

PARALLEL CHARACTERS

I think it's more fun and appropriate to parallel the actual *character* you are auditioning for rather than the musical style.

Show	Character	Song
Beauty and the Beast	Gaston	"Me"
Camelot	Lancelot	"C'est Moi"
A Little Night Music	Carl-Magnus	"In Praise of Women"
Man of La Mancha	Don Quixote	"Man of La Mancha"
Martin Guerre	Martin Guerre	"I'm Martin Guerre"
Nine	Guido	"Guido's Song"
The Pirates of Penzance	Pirate	"Pirate King"

Ingenues

Brigadoon	Fiona	"Waiting for My Dearie"
Carousel	Julie Jordan	"If I Loved You"
Guys and Dolls	Sarah Brown	"I'll Know"
How to Succeed . . .	Rosemary	"Happy to Keep His Dinner Warm"
Music Man	Marian	"My White Knight"

Ingenues (continued)

Oklahoma!	Laurey	"People Will Say We're in Love"
110 in the Shade	Lizzie	"Simple Little Things"
Plain and Fancy	Katie	"Young and Foolish"
Showboat	Julie	"Make Believe"
State Fair	Margie	"It Might As Well Be Spring"

Character/Villains/Comic

Annie	Miss Hannigan	"Little Girls"
Anyone Can Whistle	Mayoress	"Me and My Town"
Applause	Eve	"One Halloween"
Carrie	Mother	"When There's No One"
Chicago	Mama Morton	"When You're Good to Mama"
Company	Joanne	"Ladies Who Lunch"
Destry Rides Again	Frenchy	"I Hate Him"
Hello, Dolly!	Dolly	"So Long, Dearie"
How Now Dow Jones	Cynthia and Kate	"They Don't Make Them Like That Anymore"
Into the Woods	Witch	"Last Midnight"
The Little Mermaid	Ursula	"Poor Unfortunate Souls"
101 Dalmatians	Cruella	"Cruella DeVil"
Sunset Boulevard	Norma Desmond	"With One Look"
The Witches of Eastwick	The Devil	"Who's the Man?"

SHOWS GROUPED BY SUBJECT MATTER

I mentioned earlier finding songs that are stylistically correct for the show you are auditioning for. Here are lists of shows that encompass similar styles:

Country-Western Influence

Always . . . Patsy Cline
Annie Get Your Gun
The Best Little Whorehouse in Texas
Big River
Calamity Jane
Down River
Li'l Abner
Louisiana Purchase
Oklahoma!
Paint Your Wagon
Parade
The Robber Bridegroom
Seven Brides for Seven Brothers
Shenandoah
The Unsinkable Molly Brown
Urban Cowboy

War/Tragedy/Historical

Cabaret
The Civil War
Jane Eyre
Kiss of the Spider Woman
Les Misérables
Man of La Mancha
Martin Guerre
Miss Saigon
Parade
1776
Titanic

Fantasy/Fable

Anyone Can Whistle
Brigadoon
Dear World
The Fantasticks
Finian's Rainbow
On a Clear Day
Once Upon a Mattress
Peter Pan
Pippin
Wicked

Sci-Fi/Fantasy

Carrie
Forbidden Planet
Hedwig and the Angry Inch
Into the Woods
Little Shop of Horrors
Rocky Horror Picture Show
Weird Romance
Zombie Prom

Horror/Suspense

Assassins
Little Shop of Horrors
Mystery of Edwin Drood
No Way to Treat a Lady
Sweeney Todd
The Witches of Eastwick

Gay/Drag

Avenue Q
Boy Meets Boy
Chicago
Elegies
Falsettos
Hairspray
Hedwig and the Angry Inch
In Gay Company
Jesus Christ Superstar
Kiss of the Spider Woman
La Cage aux Folles
Rent
Rocky Horror Picture Show

Sugar
Three Guys Naked
Victor/Victoria
When Pigs Fly
Where's Charley?

Sports

Damn Yankees
Diamonds
The First
Promises, Promises
Wonderful Town
You're a Good Man, Charlie Brown

Teens/Children

Annie
Big
Bye, Bye, Birdie
Do Patent Leather Shoes Really Reflect Up?
Doctor Doolittle
Doonesbury
Grease
Into the Woods
Is There Life After High School?
The Me Nobody Knows
Newsies
Oliver!
Runaways
Sally Blane . . . Teenage Girl Detective
The Secret Garden
Seussical
Smile
Snoopy
Willy Wonka
You're a Good Man, Charlie Brown
Zombie Prom

Ethnic

The Apple Tree
Bar Mitzvah Boy
Children of Eden
Fiddler on the Roof
Godspell
In the Beginning

Ethnic (continued)

Jesus Christ Superstar
Joseph and the Amazing
    Technicolor Dreamcoat
Milk and Honey
Parade
Rags
The Rothschilds
Show Me Where the Good Times Are
Two by Two
Yentyl
Yours, Anne
Zorba

Circus

Barnum
Carnival
Carousel
The Fantasticks
A Funny Thing Happened
    on the Way to the Forum
The Magic Show
Merlin
Stop the World, I Want to Get Off

Asian

Flower Drum Song
The Hot Mikado
The King and I
The Mikado
Pacific Overtures
Sayonara

African American

Ain't Misbehavin'
Black and Blue
Cats
Dreamgirls
Eubie
The First
Golden Boy
Hallelujah, Baby!
House of Flowers
The Life

Once on This Island
Parade
Purlie
Ragtime
Raisin
Sarava!
Showboat
The Tap Dance Kid

Spanish/Latino

Bye, Bye, Birdie
Carmelina
Carmen Jones
Evita
Jamaica
Kiss of the Spider Woman
Man of La Mancha
Paint Your Wagon
Panama Hattie
Too Many Girls
West Side Story

Story Songs

The Baker's Wife
Children of Eden
Closer Than Ever
Falsettos
The Last Five Years
Songs for a New World
Starting Here, Starting Now
Urban Myths (Music of John Bucchino)
When Pigs Fly
Wicked
Working
. . . and the music of Heisler & Goldrich

Pop/Rock

A Chorus Line
Aida
Arthur
Aspects of Love
Blood Brothers
Carrie
Chess
Children of Eden

The Civil War
Diamonds
Doonesbury
Evita
Fame
Footloose
The Full Monty
Hair
Jekyll & Hyde
Jesus Christ Superstar
Joseph and the Amazing
    Technicolor Dreamcoat
The Lion King
Mamma Mia
Marilyn
The Me Nobody Knows
Movin' Out
Personals
Rent
Romance/Romance
Saturday Night Fever
The Scarlet Pimpernel
Smile
Song and Dance
Splendora
Starlight Express
Tick, Tick . . . BOOM!
Wicked
Working
Zanna! Don't
Zombie Prom

Marriage/Relationships
Baby
Company
Falsettos
The Goodbye Girl
I Do, I Do
I Love My Wife
I Love You, You're Perfect, Now Change
A Little Night Music
Marry Me a Little
Romance/Romance
They're Playing Our Song

Show-biz Related
A Chorus Line
A Day in Hollywood/
    A Night in the Ukraine
Babes in Arms
The Boy from Oz
Fade Out—Fade In
42nd Street
Funny Girl
Gypsy
Kiss Me, Kate
Mack & Mabel
Minnie's Boys
Nunsense
Singin' in the Rain
Summer Stock

European Settings
Cabaret
Carnival
Gigi
Grand Hotel
Irma la Douce
Jacques Brel Is Alive and Well
    and Living in Paris
Kismet
Kiss of the Spider Woman
A Little Night Music
She Loves Me
The Sound of Music
The Three Penny Opera

British
Camelot
Charlie Girl
Half a Sixpence
Jekyll & Hyde
My Fair Lady
The Mystery of Edwin Drood
Oliver!
The Secret Garden
Sweeney Todd

Outcasts/Underdogs

Angel
Assassins
Barnum
Do Patent Leather Shoes Really Reflect Up?
Hairspray
The Hunchback of Notre Dame
Is There Life After High School?
A Little Night Music
Oliver!
Passion
Side Show
Whoop-Dee-Doo

1920s–1930s Song and Dance

Anything Goes
The Boyfriend
Crazy for You
Dames at Sea
42nd Street
Little Mary Sunshine
Me and My Girl
No, No, Nannette
On Your Toes
Sugar Babies

1940s–1950s (Golden Age) Shows Now Considered Standard Musical Theater

Annie Get Your Gun
Bells Are Ringing
Brigadoon

Carousel
Damn Yankees
Guys and Dolls
The King and I
Music Man
My Fair Lady
Oklahoma!
On the Town
Once upon a Mattress
The Pajama Game
The Sound of Music
South Pacific
The Unsinkable Molly Brown
West Side Story

1960s Shows Now Considered Standard Musical Theater

A Funny Thing Happened
    on the Way to the Forum
Bye, Bye, Birdie
Camelot
Carnival
Fiddler on the Roof
Hello, Dolly!
How to Succeed in Business
    Without Really Trying
Mame
Man of La Mancha
110 in the Shade
She Loves Me
Sweet Charity

Over the last forty years, the work of many composers has not reflected the music that has been current in the pop culture. For instance, when you think of the 1960s, the first images that come to mind are hippies, drugs, Vietnam, protests, and folk and rock music—yet *Hello, Dolly!* was produced in the 1960s. Similarly, *Follies* was written in the 1970s, and *La Cage aux Folles* and *Grand Hotel* were written in the 1980s; each holds onto the traditional style of theater music in the Golden Age. Still, many composers have been strongly influenced by the pop music of their era and have notably translated it onto the Broadway stage.

Below, the left column lists shows that reflect the times in which they were written. The right column lists shows that were written at the same time, but do not reflect that time; instead they hold onto the traditional style of the Golden Age.

1960s Broadway Sound	Versus	1960s Traditional Sound
Bye, Bye, Birdie		*Cabaret*
Celebration		*Carnival*
Golden Boy		*Hello, Dolly!*
Hair		*How to Succeed . . .*
It's a Bird . . . It's a Plane . . . It's Superman		*Fiddler on the Roof*
Promises, Promises		*A Funny Thing . . .*
Your Own Thing		*Funny Girl*
Mame		*Man of La Mancha*
She Loves Me		*Unsinkable Molly Brown*
You're a Good Man, Charlie Brown		*Zorba*

1970s Broadway Sound	Versus	1970s Traditional Sound
Applause		*Annie*
Baby		*Candide*
Chorus Line, A		*Chicago*
Company		*Follies*
Evita		*A Little Night Music*
Godspell		*On the Twentieth Century*
Golden Rainbow		*The Rothschilds*
I Love My Wife		*Sugar*
I'm Getting My Act Together and Taking It on the Road		*Sweeney Todd*
Jesus Christ Superstar		*King of Hearts*
The Magic Show		*The Me Nobody Knows*
Pippin		*Seesaw*
They're Playing Our Song		*Two Gentlemen of Verona*

1980s Broadway Sound	Versus	1980s Traditional Sound
Chess		*Barnum*
Doonesbury		*Big River*
Joseph...		*City of Angels*
Les Misérables		*Grand Hotel*
March of the Falsettos		*Into the Woods*
Marilyn		*La Cage aux Folles*
Nine		*Merrily We Roll Along*
Personals		*Mystery of Edwin Drood*
Smile		*Phantom of the Opera, The*
Song and Dance		*Sunday in the Park with George*
Starlight Express		

1990s Broadway Sound	Versus	1990s Traditional Sound
Aspects of Love		*Beauty and the Beast*
Falsettoland		*City of Angels*

Jekyll and Hyde	*The Secret Garden*
Kiss of the Spider Woman	*Steel Pier*
Miss Saigon	*Titanic*
Parade	*Victor/Victoria*
Rent	*The Will Rogers Follies*
Seussical	*The Full Monty*
The Scarlet Pimpernel	*Songs for a New World*
Sunset Boulevard	*Tick, Tick . . . BOOM!*
Tommy	*The Wild Party*

USING NONTHEATER SONGS

When auditioning for a show that requires a specialty song, don't feel you have to run to musical theater songs. For example, if you have an audition for *Big River*, the audition panel will want to hear a country song. It is perfectly acceptable and often preferred that you bring in a real country song to demonstrate your sense of that style. If the show is *Grease*, bring in a true 1950s rock 'n' roll song.

In the mid-1990s, auditions were being held for the Broadway musical *Blood Brothers*. I read the character and musical breakdown in the casting notice in *Back Stage*, the New York City–based trade paper. It said that the score was written in a light rock, pop style. A vocal-coaching client of mine asked me to find him an appropriate song to sing for the audition. Rather than look through my musical theater database, I decided a Billy Joel song would be very right for this audition. I am happy to report that he was cast in the show.

PIANO-BASED POP/ROCK WRITERS

If you are considering a pop or rock song, I suggest you look for a piano-based pop/rock artist: Billy Joel, Elton John, Barry Manilow, Carly Simon, etc. Because these writers are pianists, the printed piano music will sound close to the accompaniment you are accustomed to hearing on the radio. If, however, you choose a guitar-based artist, the piano accompaniment on the printed music will not serve the audition pianist well enough to give you the sound or rhythmic pulse you are expecting to hear. True rock 'n' roll songs that are originally written for heavy guitars and drums often sound funny when arranged for the piano.

OVERUSED SONGS

If you choose to sing a song that is overused, there is always the possibility that the auditors will tune out from sheer boredom. When the music for a current and/or highly popular show is released, many actors run to purchase it. The problem is, the auditors have to listen to these songs all day. A song that was supposedly new is now suddenly overdone. On the other hand, it's refreshing for the panel to hear a great song that nobody else thought to bring in.

If once at the audition you realize your material is being sung by a lot of other performers, don't be deterred from using it. At that point, I think it's too late to change songs, especially if you chose yours to fit this particular audition. I strongly believe that your approach is going to be unique and different simply because *you* are the one taking it. Even if you hear a great, big voice in the room singing the song you are going to use, do not panic. You have to consider that the singer might be boring to watch, or perhaps is too old for the director's vision, etc. A big voice alone does not necessarily make a successful performer.

If your song accomplishes everything you want it to, then you have to use it— even if you hear it being sung by others on the day of your audition. Driving yourself crazy by looking for other songs to use at the last minute isn't worth the risk: you might forget the lyrics, or the material might not be appropriate for the style of the show for which you are auditioning. I can't stress enough that if you perform your intended song well, you should absolutely use it. Isn't the point to show yourself off at your best?

In reading this list of overused songs, please realize that a year from now, *some* of these won't be overdone anymore because new ones will have taken their place. Others are likely to continue to be overdone for years to come. Here are examples of both kinds:

"Out Here on My Own"	*Fame*
"I Don't Know How to Love Him"	*Jesus Christ Superstar*
"Popular"	*Wicked*
"My New Philosophy"	*You're a Good Man, Charlie Brown*
"On My Own"	*Les Misérables*
"Bring Him Home"	*Les Misérables*
"Stars"	*Les Misérables*
"Memory"	*Cats*
"Someone Like You"	*Jekyll & Hyde*
"This Is the Moment"	*Jekyll & Hyde*
"Corner of the Sky"	*Pippin*
"Take Me as I Am"	*Rent*
"Maybe This Time"	*Cabaret*
"Into the Fire"	*The Scarlet Pimpernel*
"Wherever He Ain't"	*Mack and Mabel*

Again, presenting yourself at your best at an audition is what's important. However, if you have gone to a lot of auditions and discovered that your song is used by many other singers, you may want to look for another song that isn't so popular, yet accomplishes the same things. If, after researching and investigating other songs, you find that the one you have been using works best for you, then you should continue to use it.

OBSCURE MATERIAL

Every singer is forever in search of a hard-to-find, obscure song to use at auditions. There are a lot of pros and cons to this search. The bottom line is, use a song that you enjoy singing and that demonstrates the skills you are trying to show the panel. If that song happens to be obscure, good, but choosing a song *solely* because it's rarely done is a miscalculation. So often I see a singer audition with an obscure song that means nothing to him or her; this person believes the panel will love it simply because it *is* obscure. To reiterate, the panel will enjoy your song only if it suits you well. Its rarity should just be a bonus.

Keep in mind, too, that many pianists may not know your obscure song. Is your manuscript handwritten, sloppy, and hard to read? Then you've sabotaged your own audition. Be careful to have a backup song in the event the pianist can't play your first choice. The panel would always prefer that you sing a well-known song well, rather than do an obscure song poorly.

RESEARCHING WRITERS

Ask yourself what theater songs you really like. What lyrics have you heard that really appeal to you? For example, if you love the music for the show *Gypsy*, find out who the composer is. You'll learn that it is Jule Styne. Look in the card catalog or computer database under Jule Styne. You will be amazed to find out that over the course of fifty years he wrote hundreds of songs, both well known and obscure, for shows and films. Among the songs are Grammy Award winners.

Did you know that aside from composing the scores for *Gypsy*, *Funny Girl*, *Bells Are Ringing*, *Hallelujah, Baby!*, *Fade Out—Fade In*, *Subways Are for Sleeping*, *Sugar*, etc., he wrote such classic songs as "Guess I'll Hang My Tears Out to Dry," "Saturday Night Is the Loneliest Night of the Week," It's Been a Long, Long Time," and "Time After Time"?

Also, I must mention that if a show by any composer or writing team is labeled a "flop," don't let that deter you from investigating some of its great songs or monologues. Its being a flop just means that the show didn't work as a whole.

CELEBRITY TYPES

My next suggestion is to find a theater personality whom you admire or think you resemble in type. For example: Bernadette Peters. If you look up Miss Peters in a theater history book, you'll find background on her career and accomplishments. I promise that you will discover she has been in shows you have never even heard of. Find those shows and listen to the recordings, or simply read through the lyrics. If the material looks interesting, but you cannot find the recording, get hold of the music (through your local library, bookstore, or music store) and have a pianist/coach tape-record it for you so you can learn it.

The more shows you do, the more actors you will meet. Find people older than you who perhaps were your type at some point. Talk to them about what material they might recommend to you.

Be open to all types of music. Material you initially dislike and resist may end up becoming your favorite.

AUDITIONING FOR A FULL SEASON

Many theaters such as regional or summer stock companies cast their entire seasons in one round of auditions. In this situation your audition material should not be targeted to one particular role for one specific production. It's also virtually impossible to find two songs that can reflect the styles of, perhaps, eight shows.

You need to demonstrate the range of your talents by presenting two contrasting songs. One should be an up-tempo and the other a ballad. The two songs need to show as much variety as possible in both vocal (pop, blues, jazz, standard, etc.) and acting range. The casting people should see a contrast in dramatic content, period, and style. If your two songs aren't written by the same author(s) and aren't from the same decade, their styles are more likely to differ. Again, the more varied and contrasting your material, the wider range of skills you will be able to show the panel.

CHAPTER 2

Who Said Musical Theater Actors Can't Act?

For a musical theater performer, knowing how to "act" is as important as knowing how to sing and dance. This chapter defines acting terminology, and briefly delves into the basics of "how to."

Unfortunately, a stigma is associated with musical theater performers: they are not thought to be true actors. I strongly disagree with this. Admittedly, many scripts (a.k.a. librettos) for musicals aren't always written in great depth—because in a musical, a song or dance expresses what would be conveyed by a scene in a play. So why not just sing the song or dance the dance? Because a well-crafted theater song may be written to sound beautiful, but conveying its beauty is only a part of the singer's job. To be a vibrant, vital element of the show, the song must be performed by an actor who understands the craft of creating an emotional journey. Otherwise his or her performance is merely a dull presentation of a lovely song.

Over the last fifteen years, theater composers and lyricists have become more sophisticated in their writing, requiring singers who are well-trained, dynamic actors. Hopefully, the old stigma will soon become a thing of the past.

THE MOMENT BEFORE

As part of your rehearsal process, you need to find and define for yourself "the moment before" your audition song begins. Ask yourself why you need to say these words or to pose these questions in the lyric right now, dramatically speaking. Why not last night, or two weeks from now? What *is* the moment before? What specifically just kicked you in the butt to make you emote at this instant? Possibilities could be a phone call, reading a letter from your ex-boyfriend, a conversation, old photos, finding his or her things, or scratching off a winning lottery ticket.

Never wait for the musical introduction to end before you start to act. Use the piano introduction as your time to be in the moment before. If, instead, you need to be in the moment before *prior* to the piano introduction, you'll have to give the pianist a simple cue as to when to begin playing. When you first meet the pianist, for example, you can say, "Please start playing when I lift my head."

"DOING"

Acting is "doing," and I'm not necessarily referring to physical "doing." *Living* is the kind of doing I want to focus on here. If I were speaking this text aloud to a class, I would naturally be playing such actions as to teach, to inform, to explain, to clarify, to reiterate, or to emphasize.

Just as in real life, an action propels the words you say—or sing—onstage or at an audition. When choosing actions to play for your lyrics, avoid verbs that are too ambiguous or too passive. Otherwise your performance will become so passive and internal that it can't be shared with your audience or with your imaginary scene partner.

You can actively play verbs like to lure, to seduce, to celebrate, to ask, to beg, to thank, to educate, and to confess—because they are active. It is more difficult to play verbs like to remember, to think, to tell, and to try, because these verbs are not active enough. I urge you to find stronger ones.

Don't confuse verbs with adjectives and adverbs. (Examples include "I am a desperate man" and "I am desperate.") Desperate, angry, elated, sad, and shy are *feelings*, not actions. Adjectives and adverbs cannot be played; instead they are the *result* of playing actions and verbs.

While I was clarifying, reiterating, and emphasizing this text for a class, I might have become frustrated or excited. Those emotions grew naturally out of the situation—from the class's response to my teaching, from the physical condition of the room (too hot, too light), or from what I was doing before I entered the room. I didn't begin my lecture by feeling, but by taking a specific action. A singer who spends the sixteen bars of his or her audition feeling emotions is probably an untrained and unseasoned actor. If you know what you are talking about, whom you are talking to, and why, your emotions will naturally be there.

FIND INTERESTING ACTIONS

A great exercise for finding actions is to change the situation of your song—to do an improvisation. Take a song such as "If I Loved You" from *Carousel* and try singing it to your dog. Or pretend that you are not allowed to love the person romantically because you are a nun, or deliver these lyrics as if you have just been released from jail after two years.

Let yourself be free to explore many different approaches. You will be surprised at how many new actions come about.

PACE YOUR ACTIONS

If your song is about convincing your wife not to leave you, I suggest not starting with actions like begging or pleading, because those verbs are what I refer to as severe actions. How can you possibly top them? I would start with actions like suggesting, considering, clarifying, apologizing, offering, and joking; then you can work your way up to begging or pleading.

If, for instance, your song is about asking your boyfriend to marry you, the journey of the song would end immediately if your first action were to come right out and ask—unless, of course, the lyrics start that way. Find actions like hinting, joking, reminding, etc. These actions make for an interesting journey as the audition panel or the audience watches you find the courage to propose. Actions should intensify to aid in accomplishing your objective.

OBJECTIVE

Actions, not feelings, lead you to an objective. To help find the overall intention or objective of a song, try to figure out the author's reasoning for writing it in this scene and for this character. What does the song accomplish for the story of the play? What does it help the audience to understand? Does the song work outside the context of the show? Why wasn't this sentiment simply written as a scene without music? How can you personally relate to the given situation?

For instance, in the show *City of Angels*, there is a scene in which a character sneaks into a detective's apartment looking for something. As she is snooping around, the detective walks in and catches her. Her objective is established immediately: how to get out of this situation without being brought down to the police station.

She tries to accomplish her objective by playing actions like distracting, seducing, joking around, lying, apologizing, and finally begging and pleading. Whether or not the character does achieve her objective is dictated by the script. In either case, the actress must know what that objective is, and do everything she can to accomplish it.

JOURNEY

Is there any sort of transformation or change in your character from the beginning of the song to the end? If so, where? Is your song a discovery song that needs to unfold as the piece unfolds? If so, the panel and/or audience need to see it unravel as you do. Is this song a response to an incident, a response to something someone has said, or both? Is this a question song? Is there a great need to get an answer out of someone (your imaginary scene partner)? Whatever type of song you're singing, you must learn how to pace the journey so that it ends when the song does.

DON'T GIVE IT AWAY

Be careful not to play the ending at the beginning of the piece—don't play the results. Even though you have rehearsed and memorized your song, your *character* cannot appear to be too knowing. In your character's reality, he or she is finding and speaking these words for the first time. If you can learn to perform the song each time as if it is the first time, then your presentation will always be honest and genuine. If you try to fake your performance, the audition panel will see through it. You can't present, act, feel, or perform "truth." Truth can only come from you, the actor, preparing your song and knowing what the journey and objective is, yet not allowing your character to know the future. The auditors should never see you acting. Instead they should only see, as famed acting teacher Sanford Meisner put it, a person living in an imaginary circumstance.

PHYSICALITY

When it comes to addressing the issue of physicality in an audition, a question commonly asked is, "Can I move around, or do I need to stand still while presenting my song?" It's important that I make it clear that there are no set rules! Your decision should be based on the type of song you are using. If your up-tempo song, for instance, is bouncy, rhythmic, celebratory, or presentational, then standing still would probably seem unnatural.

By a "presentational song," I mean one that is sung to the world or to the audience. "I Met a Girl" from *Bells Are Ringing* is a guy's response to meeting the most beautiful girl he's ever seen. In the song's original staging, he came out of a subway station shouting to everyone on the streets that he just met a girl. A similar example of a presentational song is "I'm in Love With a Wonderful Guy" from *South Pacific*. Again, the song was originally blocked leaving the character, Nellie, alone onstage, celebrating her new love interest. Blocking refers to an actor's physical activity onstage. For example, a director might tell an actor to walk downstage to a table, pick up a glass, and sit on a chair nearby.

In presenting a ballad, I would suggest limiting your need to walk around. I will make a generalization by stating that the majority of ballads are either love songs or self-discovery songs. Therefore, singing to the world would be inappropriate. In this case, singing either to an imaginary person, like your boyfriend, or to yourself would be more appropriate. In the song "Marry Me" from *The Rink*, the character is proposing to the girl he has always had a crush on. In the song "Before I Gaze at You" from *Camelot*, Guinevere sings directly to Lancelot.

One of the biggest traps to avoid is not deciding ahead of time what kind of physical movement you are going to use. When first learning a song, allow your body to respond to the music naturally, not worrying about whether it's too much for an audition. Once you have experienced the sensation of letting go, cut out any excessive movement you think will be considered going too far—without forgetting how it felt to let go.

When I hear the song "I Met a Girl," I want to run around the room and jump onto a chair, so I can tell the whole world what just happened to me. Knowing that jumping on furniture might scare the auditors, I would tone down some of the physicalization, while still holding onto the feeling I had when I was able to jump around. My energy and excitement would be so obvious that in fact I would probably almost seem to be running and jumping around.

TELEVISED TALENT CONTESTS

Be careful not to seek good acting on television programs such as *Star Search* and *American Idol*. These competitive shows are very performance oriented. They are not about performers demonstrating their ability to act, but rather about their ability to sing and sell a song to an audience. Most of the singers only play and display emotions, thinking they are acting.

WHO ARE YOU FAVORITE PERFORMERS?

Who are some of the artists that you emulate, and why? What about them captures your attention? After reading this chapter, examine your response to musical performers from an educated actor's point of view. Do they only have great voices, or are they also actors who live in the moment? Do they invite you to go on a journey with them, or do they bore you so much that you are only thinking about where to eat after the show?

Checklist

Here is a condensed checklist for this chapter.

Preparation

- What is the context in which the song was written?
- How do you relate to the situation?
- Are you talking to yourself, to the audience, or to an imaginary person?
- What is the journey?
- What actions do you need to play?
- Do you need to add any physicalization?
- What is the overall objective of the song?

Acting

- Leave all of your preparation at home. If you have prepared well, that information will be stored in your brain and you won't have to think about it.
- Remind yourself of your objective.
- Determine the moment before you start.
- Remind yourself what the journey/arc is before you begin.
- Allow your character to live in the moment and to take the journey for the first time.

CHAPTER 3

Defining Sixteen Bars

When a show is being cast, often there will be what is called an "open call," or a "chorus call." These auditions are open to anyone who wants to attend (including my grandmother, who can't sing). On any given day of a chorus call, the auditors might be faced with having to see 300 to 400 singers. To ensure that everyone can be seen (though it's not *always* possible), the "sixteen-bar" formula was created.

FORM

Although sixteen bars does mean sixteen measures of music, many auditors interpret the sixteen-bar formula as a feel, the reason being that for so many decades, a "song" was written in a familiar structure. The most well known of these is the "AABA" form—"A" being the verse and "B" being the bridge (a.k.a. the release). Having the AABA structure made constructing sixteen bars a very straightforward process: start with the bridge and end with the verse.

Some theater composers still write using the AABA form, but a lot of new composers do not. Many musical scores are now "through-composed," meaning scenes are actually sung instead of spoken. Hence, the familiar formula has been broken. Even today, when a "song" is written for a show, "C," "D," and "E" sections are often added to it.

Finding the best sixteen bars is difficult because not only do you want to find a section that shows off your voice; you also want to find a section of the lyric that still makes dramatic sense and allows you to find a logical journey.

In any format, using material from the beginning of a song doesn't show much range, merely due to the fact that the music and lyrics haven't had a chance to develop. The turning point or climax of most songs, dramatically and musically, happens about three-quarters of the way through. Therefore, presenting the climax with a resolve at the end of the song shows the greatest range of your skills.

CONSTRUCTING SIXTEEN BARS

The current "norms" for a sixteen-bar cut are ballads lasting no more than thirty seconds, and up-tempos lasting no more than thirty-five seconds (because an up-tempo naturally feels faster). About seventy percent of today's auditors will allow you this much time. Unfortunately, the other thirty percent still insist that "sixteen bars" is definitely and only sixteen measures of music, and will cut you off after your sixteenth measure.

As discussed in the beginning of this chapter, sixteen bars is often more a feel than an exact science. If your up-tempo song, for instance, is written in cut time (which means double time), then singing sixteen bars would only last about fifteen seconds. Therefore, you can use thirty-two bars to reach the thirty- to thirty-five-second limit. If you are still questioning the length of your sixteen-bar cut, then actually time it with a stopwatch or a clock that has a second hand.

NO ROAD SIGNS

Your sixteen-bar cut should not have any extraneous music on the page. Literally cut and paste your music so the pianist can read straight ahead without having to jump around the page following arrows as road signs.

Since your sixteen bars of music are usually not taken from the beginning of the song, you must remember to transfer the following information to the page where you are beginning your audition cut. You can either rewrite this information, or cut and paste it onto what is now your starting page:

1. Song title

2. Composer's and lyricist's names

3. Name of show or film that the song is from (if any)

4. Tempo marking

5. Musical style (jazz, waltz, swing, soft-shoe, tango, rumba, etc.)

6. Key signature

7. Musical introduction—clearly marked

WHAT, EXACTLY, DO SIXTEEN BARS ACCOMPLISH?

Believe it or not, they allow the audition panel to learn the following immediately:

1. Your general sense of musicality (phrasing, style, dynamics)

2. Your physical appearance (height, body type, age, look)

3. The power of your voice

4. Your personality

5. Your understanding of lyrics (acting)

6. Intonation, meaning pitch problems (singing sharp or flat)

7. Whether you have any speech impediments (e.g., lisp, stutter)

You have *got* to be kidding!

MUSICAL INTRODUCTIONS

Every song needs some kind of musical lead-in to help you find your first note—and to allow you some time to prepare emotionally. What is going to help you establish the tempo or beat? What will help establish the mood? Most often the intro already exists in the music. If not, have a friend who reads music or a vocal coach write one in for you. I would suggest using the shortest possible introduction. You don't want your sixteen-bar song to have a four-bar lead-in, especially if the auditors are being strict about time.

The introduction should be tailored to your needs. How you begin your song instantly either grabs or loses the panel's interest. There are four musical introduction options to choose from:

1. Bell tone—using the first pitch of your song as the introduction

2. Arpeggio—using a rolled chord

3. Open vamp—playing a phrase that keeps repeating until you are ready to start singing

4. Set number of bars—always hearing the same phrase to help you get your first note

UP-TEMPOS SHOULD START WITH A RHYTHMIC VAMP OR A SET NUMBER OF BARS

Having a rhythmic introduction helps set the pulse and feel the beat and actual tempo of an up-tempo song. I like to think of a vamp as a moving sidewalk. Once the pianist starts playing, it's up to you to jump in when ready. If the pianist is playing the wrong tempo during the introduction, this is a good time to stop him or her.

BALLADS SHOULD START WITH A BELL TONE OR AN ARPEGGIO

A ballad is usually not set in a specific tempo. It generally has a give-and-take, "follow-the-singer" approach. Therefore, a rhythmic introduction with a ballad would not be appropriate or helpful to you. A one-note lead-in (bell tone) or an arpeggio (rolled chord) would be better.

MUSICAL ENDINGS

If the sheet music is not written the way you want your cut to end, then you need to adjust the page by writing in the changes, or by having your coach or anyone who reads music write them in. Remember, the ending of the song needs to be just as strong as the beginning because it's the last thing your auditors will hear.

ENDING OPTIONS

If your sixteen-bar cut ends too abruptly, without a sense of finality, you can make the following changes in the music:

1. *Extend the musical rideout.* Have your pianist or coach add more music at the end, so that you can sustain the final note.

2. *Shorten the musical rideout.* If the held note is too long for you to sustain at the end of the song, have your pianist or coach cut out some of the music.

3. *Create an ending that matches your physical "button."* Your performance needs to end dramatically and physically at the same time. This lets the panel know that you have finished.

A STRONG BUTTON

A button is the final note and moment of a song, both musically and physically. Whether the button is a sung note or is played by the pianist, it must clearly inform the listener that you are done. Think of the button as physicalizing the final punctuation, e.g., the period, exclamation point, or question mark.

One helpful way to find a strong button is to ask yourself, if there were one more word at the end of the song, what would it be? Would it be "Yes!," "Nope," "Whew," "So there!," or "I dare you!"? Once you come up with the word, physicalize it.

Be sure your musical and physical buttons time out together. You don't want to sustain the final note longer than there is music for the pianist to play. If you haven't adjusted your button to fit your needs, the panel will assume that you have never rehearsed this song with the actual written music.

Composer-lyricist Jerry Herman says the ending of a song is the most important part because it is what the audience remembers most. The listeners want to know when they can applaud.

SUMMING UP

Approaching sixteen bars as an actor should not be any different than approaching a full song. Even though you may only be asked to sing sixteen bars, you must still convey a beginning, middle, and end. Once you have found the journey of your song in its full length, figure out how to condense it into your sixteen-bar cut. It is imperative that you do learn the *entire* song first. If it appears to the auditors that you really don't understand the lyrics, you risk the chance of becoming known as the singer who cannot act. Singing well may get you work in the chorus, but it's not likely to land you a leading role that requires a trained actor.

CHAPTER 4

The Condition of Your Music

It is important to create a binder that will keep your audition music together. Not only will it prevent losing pages, but it will keep your music neat, orderly, and ready to go.

NO LOOSE PAGES, PLEASE

Loose pages of music have a way of flying off the piano, blown by a breeze from an open window or a nearby ceiling fan. Keep your music in a three-ring binder to avoid this. Try to eliminate as many page turns as possible for the pianist. If your song is four pages long, for example, the pianist should not have to turn four pages. Tape pages two and three back-to-back (or print the pages double-sided) so there is only one page turn.

If you like putting the pages of your music in plastic covering, be sure to purchase nonglare plastic sheets. Otherwise, the pianist may see only his or her reflection from the fluorescent lights or the sun hitting the plastic.

Many actors like to tape the pages of their music together instead of using a three-ring binder. I don't recommend doing that because, as I've just mentioned, a breeze can blow your pages off the piano. Also, many old pianos (often found at some audition sites) do not have backboards to set your music on.

UNUSED MARKINGS

Erase all extraneous markings on your music: breath marks, chord symbols from someone else's transposition, ritards, etc. Whenever you get a piece of music from a friend, make sure that any added notations do not conflict with your interpretation.

In one audition that I played at, a woman handed me her music, explained the tempo of her song, and walked away from the piano. Before I had the chance to ask her a question about the music, she began singing. As I was sight-reading the music, I saw a breath mark highlighted, so I obeyed the marking. The singer turned to me and asked why I had taken a breath/pause on that musical phrase. I said it was marked that way in the music. Very defensively she told me it wasn't her marking.

Well, how was I supposed to know that? She should have either gotten a clean copy of the song or whited out any markings that were not hers.

My favorite story is of the young woman who put her music down on the piano and proceeded to walk to the center of the room. I stopped her because I noticed there were chord symbols for three different keys above the music. Mind you, each of the three keys was highlighted with a different color marker. I asked her which key she wanted me to play the song in and she replied that she didn't know. Being the wise guy that I am, I said, well, we have three options: the blue, the red, and the yellow key. She didn't laugh. She told me her vocal coach never told her, therefore she thought the music was clear for the pianist to read. It took us two tries around the piano—in the middle of her audition—till we settled on an appropriate key. (We chose blue, in case you would like to know.)

NEW MARKINGS

Do highlight important markings such as ritards, key changes, meter changes, etc., that you *are* going to observe. If your interpretation of a song is different from the written music, then you need to notate the differences clearly. When handed a well-known song, a pianist likely will not pay too much attention to details because he or she has probably played it a hundred times. Therefore, you need to make the pianist aware of your changes by actually writing them in the music. I even suggest going so far as highlighting the changes and additions (with a yellow highlighter) so there is less room for error.

The two safest steps you can take are to give the pianist your changes verbally and to mark them in the music in case he or she forgets what you just said.

WRONG KEYS

One of the biggest mistakes you can ever make during your audition is to find out that your song is written in the wrong key for you. A pianist should never be expected to transpose your music on sight. Remember: it's your audition, not the pianist's.

Never assume that the vocal selection books you buy at your local music store will have the same arrangement or be in the same key as the cast recording. Only the original musical score will parallel the cast album. The same rule applies to pop songs: published sheet music is rarely in the key performed by the original artist. Always be sure to rehearse with a pianist—or even with a pitch pipe, if that's the best you can do—to find out the key. Also be aware of the fact that with so many revivals on Broadway, new cast recordings may not coincide with the key of the original score.

The very last thing that should cause you any surprises is *your* music. It is the one element over which you can and should have control.

WRONG LYRICS

White out all unused lyrics. If you are using the last sixteen bars of a five-page song as your sixteen-bar cut but you decide to use the lyrics from an earlier part of the song, then you need to white out or paste over the unused lyrics and write in the ones you are singing. This way, the pianist will be able to follow you better. Otherwise, if the pianist is distracted for a moment, then looks back at the music to find his or her place and you are singing lyrics other than those written, confusion can result and the pianist may believe he or she is playing in the wrong place.

EXTRA COPIES

When you've completed all of the instructions above, make several copies of your finished cut-and-paste job. Now that you've done all that arts-and-crafts work, it would be a shame to have to start all over again because you lost your music or spilled something on it.

CHAPTER 5

Before the Audition

After a while auditioning will become routine, as it becomes a part of your everyday life. But every audition must be treated as respectfully as your first. It is too easy to fall into the trap of "going through the motions."

TEN PITFALLS

1. Not deciding what to wear to suggest the style/milieu of the show
2. Not going to sleep at a reasonable hour
3. Not deciding what to sing ahead of time
4. Not eating breakfast before you leave for the audition
5. Not bringing water and perhaps a snack to eat in case you have to wait for hours to be seen
6. Not realizing you need an umbrella
7. Not knowing exactly where the audition site is located
8. Not putting extra headshots and résumés in your binder
9. Not warming up (physically and vocally)
10. Not turning your cell phone off

LOCATE THE AUDITION SITE

It is very important to learn where all of the popular audition sites around your city are. Don't wait until the morning of your audition to find out where it is located. New facilities open and close all the time, so keep an eye out. Resources include the national Theatre Communications Group and local service organizations like the New Jersey Theatre Alliance, the Austin (Texas) Circle of Theaters, and the League of Washington (D.C.) Theatres, which list member companies' addresses. Publications and their corresponding Web sites (like *Back Stage* in New York, *PerformInk* in Chicago, and *Back Stage West* in Los Angeles) carry display and/or classified ads for theater and rehearsal space rentals, as well as relevant news items.

WARM UP

Before getting to the audition site, take care of any vocal and physical warm-ups that you require. There is simply no room on location that could possibly accommodate the gymnastics of hundreds of auditionees.

EAT SOMETHING

Pardon me for sounding like your mother, but do make sure you eat before leaving home. You don't know how long you may have to wait before you actually audition. Your body needs fuel for energy, so bring a snack and a bottle of water with you, just in case.

BRING HEADSHOTS AND RÉSUMÉS

Make sure that you bring several headshots and up-to-date résumés to every audition. It is very common for someone on the panel to ask for extra copies for upcoming projects that you might be right for. Also, the casting director may want extras for his or her files.

LEAVE EARLY

When you leave your home, allow plenty of time for handling traffic and subway delays. It is far better to be early than to be running in five minutes before you have to sing.

This may sound overcautious, but if you need cash, don't wait until you are on your way to an audition to find a cash machine. The one ATM near your home will most likely be out of service when you are in a rush.

THINK ABOUT YOUR CLOTHES

Choose clothing that you feel comfortable wearing. Please dress your age and don't try to look like someone you are not. Dressing in costume for the character you are auditioning for is totally unnecessary and is usually discouraged, though your choices can certainly *suggest* the style or period of the piece. For example, women auditioning for a show set in the 1920s or 1930s should wear heels and makeup, and probably put their hair up. On the other hand, performers of either sex who are auditioning for *Rent* or *Hair* would probably be smart to wear jeans and sneakers.

It is *not* advisable to wear accessories such as nose and tongue rings—especially if you are auditioning for a period show. If you reek "contemporary," it can be difficult for an auditor to imagine you as anything else.

It's a good idea always to have street clothes to change back into after your audition. Some actors try to set aside one or two outfits to use exclusively for auditions, so they are clean and ready to go at any time. What you wear says a lot about you. Put some thought into it.

Remember, an audition is about you and your talents, not about your ability to shop for clothes and accessories. What you wear on your own time is your choice. At an audition you want to appear somewhat neutral and moldable, while still displaying a sense of individuality. Have fun shopping!

Suggested Attire for Men at a Singing/Acting Audition

These Work

- Sport jacket with a sweater

- Shirt and tie

- Shirt and tie without a jacket

- Vest and tie without a jacket

- Nice pants or khakis (with a belt)

- Jeans, if they look clean

- Clean shoes

These Don't

- Don't wear sneakers unless they're appropriate for the show (e.g., *Grease, West Side Story, Rent, Tick, Tick . . . BOOM!*, and *Hair*).

- Try not to wear all black if possible; it doesn't say much about your personality, and many other performers will be wearing black.

- Makeup is not necessary.

Suggested Attire for Women at a Singing/Acting Audition

These Work

- Makeup—but not stage makeup

- An outfit that flatters your figure, preferably a skirt or casual dress—it's a good idea to allow the panel to see your legs—but pants are certainly acceptable if they are more comfortable for you, if your movement requires them, or if they're more appropriate for the show

- Heels—especially when auditioning for a period show when heels were the norm

These Don't

- Accessories are okay, but keep them to a minimum. Be sure they are secure; you don't want them dangling or falling off during the audition.

- Make sure your jewelry doesn't reflect the light; this could become very distracting for the panelists.

- Try to stay away from wearing all black; it can often make you look very pale, and it says little about your personality.

READ THE CASTING NOTICE CAREFULLY!

When the Broadway musical *Starlight Express* was holding auditions in New York City several years ago, the casting director noticed that almost everyone waiting in line to audition was wearing roller skates. Yes, the show requires that all actors be able to demonstrate great skill in roller skating, yet the ad hadn't asked for skates at this time. The casting director needed to first find out who could sing and act *without* wheels. Once those people were chosen, they would be called back to roller-skate.

A similar situation took place during auditions for the premiere of *La Cage aux Folles* on Broadway. Most of the male actors arrived in drag because everyone knew that the show called for it. Again, the casting director needed to find out first who could act, sing, and dance *without* heels. Those called back were asked to dress in drag (with heels).

Always read the casting notice carefully, and remember that the panel needs to see your basic skills—acting, singing, and dancing—before adding any others. You can't furnish a new house before the foundation is built.

CHAPTER 6

You've Arrived!

Congratulations on finding the audition site (theater, union hall, rehearsal studio . . .) and arriving with plenty of time to catch your breath. At a non-Equity (non-union) audition, you will probably see a fair amount of chaos. Actors will be running around asking questions such as, "How long do I have to wait?" "Are they running behind?" "How many songs do they want to hear?" "How's the pianist? "Hey, can you do lunch afterwards?" "Who did your headshots?"

Focus, take a deep breath, and listen for instructions. Once you sign in at a non-Equity chorus call, you will usually be given an audition number. If so, remember it, as it will be your number for the remainder of the day.

Once you become a member of Actors' Equity Association (the union with jurisdiction over principals, chorus members, and stage managers in "legitimate" theater), the audition process is much more organized and controlled.

COMMON COURTESY

While waiting to audition, don't annoy those around you. Your call may be two hours from now, but the person sitting next to you could be going on in ten minutes. Some actors like to concentrate and prepare; some get very nervous and don't want to be social and chatty until they have finished their auditions. Be respectful of them, as you would want them to be of you.

TYPING OUT

If there is a large turnout, the director may decide to "type out." This is a means for the audition panel to eliminate hundreds of people at an overcrowded audition, simply by looking at their physical types and résumés.

Is this considered rude? No, not at all. If the director is looking to cast a specific type and you do not fit that type, why wait around wasting your time and his or hers? If you are definitely too old, or too short, or too heavy for this particular director's vision, you may as well know right away so you can run errands, get back to work, or even go to another audition.

An example of typing out that comes to mind is Tommy Tune's auditions for the Broadway revival of *Grease* in the mid-1990s. At that time, I was teaching a musical theater audition class. Many of my students were in their early twenties, so when they heard of these auditions, most of them thought they had a great chance of being seen. All of them worked very hard to prepare, and many of them had to take a day off from work to attend the audition. What they and I didn't know was that Tommy Tune was casting this production with actors in their mid-to-late twenties, and even into their thirties. None of my students got to sing for Mr. Tune. They were all typed out instantly because they looked too young.

KNOW FOR WHOM YOU ARE AUDITIONING

Find out specifically for whom you are auditioning. If it's not listed in the ad or if it's not posted on the door when you arrive, ask the audition monitor. You must start learning the names of working directors, musical directors, choreographers, and casting directors, for you're likely to be auditioning for them again soon.

A friend of mine called for advice on how to prepare for an important callback. I asked her who the director was, and she had no idea. "How can you not know who called you back?" I asked her.

It never ceases to amaze me how any actor can audition for a show with no knowledge of who is in the room running the audition. Whether or not you actually book the job, if you sense that the director is interested in you, you should find out that person's name. The next time you read on a casting Web site or in a trade paper that this person is directing another show, run to that audition!

WHO IS USUALLY SITTING BEHIND THE AUDITION TABLE?

For a musical audition, the director, choreographer, and musical director are present throughout the entire casting process. Regional theaters, summer stock companies, dinner theaters, etc., usually confine their auditions to one week. For those auditions the people above plus the producer are present—because, ultimately, this person will have the final say.

If you are auditioning for a new show, you can be sure that you'll see the writers behind the table, as well as those mentioned above. However, since the audition process on a Broadway production can last for months, most of the artistic staff won't be present until the casting director has weeded out everyone not appropriate for the show.

At an Equity or non-Equity "chorus call" for a Broadway production, Broadway replacement, or Broadway national tour, most often the casting director and pianist are the only ones in the room, at least for the first few rounds of auditions. The casting director's function is to narrow the field by eliminating any performer who definitely does not fit the needs of the show, either physically or vocally. After having spent the week seeing anywhere from 500 to 700 people, the casting director will keep seventy-five to one hundred of them on file, to be seen again by the creative team. Usually directors or authors of high status, like Hal Prince or Stephen Sondheim, are not present until the final callbacks—sometimes weeks or months after the casting process began.

For an Equity principal audition (EPA), the above would also apply. (So would the request for a sixteen-bar cut.) Only those performers interested in auditioning for a principal role attend an EPA call. Singers and dancers who think they are right only for the ensemble of that show attend a chorus call. If you go to a chorus call and the casting director is really interested in you for a principal role, he or she will call you back for the principals' callbacks.

Note that actors who are submitted to audition by the casting director do not need to attend any of the open calls. Those actors are given an appointment to audition on a different day.

COMBINED AUDITIONS: WHAT ARE THEY, AND WHO ATTENDS?

Combined auditions offer performers the opportunity to audition for dozens of theater companies, all at one time. These events are held regionally throughout the country, usually every spring, and can be attended by representatives of all kinds of theaters, from summer stock companies to outdoor dramas to dinner theaters to theme parks.

There are literally dozens of combined auditions. To give you some idea of how they're organized, this section focuses on two examples: StrawHat Auditions and the New England Theater Conference (NETC).

StrawHat Auditions

These are held in New York City, usually in March, to cast for all participating summer stock companies located in the eastern region of the country. Although StrawHat is "an organization that supports the careers of non-Equity actors," a number of Equity theaters seeking Membership Candidates, interns, and second-company performers attend these auditions also.

Application and Fee You can find an audition application by going to the StrawHat Web site at www.strawhat-auditions.com. The deadline for returning the application is mid-February, but if you wait too long to send it in, all of the slots might already be filled. A $40.00 application fee goes toward the cost of the audition space, audition pianist, etc. If you have applied too late or are screened out, your fee is returned.

What to Prepare Performers have ninety seconds to present two pieces. Singers are asked to present a song first, followed by a monologue. Nonsingers are asked to prepare two monologues. Callbacks are posted regularly throughout the day.

New England Theater Conference

This organization bills itself as "New England's oldest, largest regional theatre association." As many as forty to seventy theater companies participate in the annual March auditions, which are open to non-Equity members and Equity Membership

Candidates. (The EMC Program is described in Chapter 22, "Getting Experience," page 39). You can find more information online at www.netconline.org.

Application and Fee In 2005 the audition fee for NETC members was $30, for students $45.00, and for nonstudents, $55.00. Application forms are available in November of the previous year. Unlike StrawHat, the application fee is nonrefundable, whether or not the performer receives an audition slot.

What to Prepare Performers have a total of two minutes to present their material. Singers should prepare one song and one monologue, or two contrasting songs. (An accompanist is provided.) Nonsingers should prepare two monologues. Each hour, a list is posted with the names of actors that have been called back.

If you get called back by at least ten percent of the participating theaters at any combined audition, then attending was probably worthwhile.

PROS AND CONS

Attending large auditions has its pluses and minuses. On the plus side is the time that you save by not having to audition for these theaters separately.

One major reservation that I have about combined auditions is that you have to apply by mail to be seen. The application fees probably bother me the most. Yes, the money covers the cost of the audition studios, pianists, advertising, and processing, but I still have a problem with the idea of an actor having to pay to audition. However, if you have the money to spend, it certainly can't hurt to attend.

You can find combined theater auditions in various regions of the country—by networking within your own theater community, reading local and trade newspapers, and checking out theater Web sites across the United States. Every January, *Back Stage* newspaper and BackStage.com publish a nationwide list and profiles of about twenty of these auditions.

THE PANEL'S POINT OF VIEW

Here's a news flash!!! The audition panel needs to hire actors, singers, and dancers in order to put on a musical. They want each person who walks through the door to be the performer they have been waiting for.

Casting is a tedious process for all involved. Try to remember that the auditors are running a business, as much as they are trying to be artistically sensitive and polite to you. They are also human beings—sometimes tired, hungry, worried, or discouraged human beings. If they ever appear unfriendly, don't take it too personally.

TRUST WHO YOU ARE

Learn to be aware of the persona that you project. For instance, actors who are shy, nervous, but very focused, can often walk into an audition appearing standoffish when they don't mean to be at all. I am not insinuating that actors should walk in acting phony in an attempt to please the panel. What I do mean to stress is that what the auditors see from the moment you walk in the door is all they have to go on. In auditions, first impressions are formed very quickly, as in any real-life situation. Think about it: when you attend a party, why are you drawn to some people immediately, but not to others?

On the day of your audition it may be ninety-nine degrees outside and crowded and stuffy inside; you may have to wait for three hours before your name is called; and you may have just broken up with your partner. Well, too bad! You must learn to leave all of that personal drama outside the audition room. If you are cast in a show, its director will expect you to leave your personal problems outside the rehearsals and performances, also. This is all part of being an actor.

SICK DAYS

Walking into an audition feeling ill and making excuses for yourself puts your auditors in a very awkward position. They are there to assess your talents and skills. Their job is not to imagine what you might sound like without a head cold. If you are not at your best, then do not go. It is only valuable for the panel to see you when you are unquestionably castable.

If an agent has submitted you, but you are ill, you should call your agent as soon as possible so that he or she can tell the panel not to expect you at the audition. If you have an audition appointment and realize en route that you aren't feeling well, try to attend to let the casting director or director know you are ill and unable to sing that day, and that you didn't want to be irresponsible by standing him or her up. Whenever possible, the casting office, along with your agent, will reschedule your appointment for another day.

KNOW YOUR MATERIAL

Really know your material! There should never be any musical surprises in your own music that could throw you off. Nerves can cause certain problems and the panel will take this into consideration, but there are *no* excuses for singing wrong notes and rhythms. How can you be counted on in a performance if you can't get through a sixteen-bar audition?

When the pianist plays the introduction to your song and you can't find your first note, it tells the musical director that you either have a weak musical ear or did not prepare properly. In neither case would this person want you in the show.

Am I allowed at least one carry-on?

WORK ETHIC

The creative team is seeking team players: actors who can be trusted, and who are willing to roll up their sleeves and work hard. If this is a new show, the authors will want someone who will work well with others and adapt well to lots of changes. They also will want someone whom they can trust with the material that they have been working on for a very long time.

If you can't adequately perform sixteen bars of a song that you've presumably chosen because you liked it and it shows your strength, and which you may well have worked on for months—why should the creative team trust you with a complete score that's new to you and which you've only ten days to rehearse?

BRING IT ALL

The panel may be very interested in you, but needs to hear a different type of song than the one you've just presented. The worst response you can give is, "I didn't bring the rest of my music with me." All of your audition music should be kept in one binder and brought to every audition. I cannot stress this enough! No matter what the ad called for, you must be ready to show the casting people more if asked. This can be the deciding factor in getting a callback or in being cast. I have never understood why singers don't keep all of their audition material together in one binder, ready to go at all times.

GO WITH THE FLOW

Do not assume that you will always get to sing two sixteen-bar songs, even though the casting notice asked for them. If the auditions are running late, the panel may only want to hear one song. Usually the monitor will alert you of this before you enter the room.

After you have completed your first song, wait until you are told what to do next. Nothing is more embarrassing for an actor than to nod to the pianist to begin playing a second song before the auditors have asked to hear it. Maybe they do not want to hear another one because they already know you are not what they are looking for. Or perhaps you were terrific and it only took that one song to get a callback.

DECISIONS

If you did not know ahead of time that the panel only wants to hear one song, but you've prepared two because that's what the casting notice requested, which one should you sing: the up-tempo or the ballad? Ask yourself which song is more appropriate for the show for which you are auditioning. When in doubt, choose the song that really shows off the strength and range of your voice. Your aim is to "wow" them enough that they want to see and hear more of you at the callbacks. I also think your first song choice should make them want to hear your second song.

If you do get to sing both songs, which one should you start with? If singing one of them makes you more nervous, then do the easier one first to help yourself relax.

Women, if you are singing a belt song and a legit soprano song—which is easier vocally to switch to? Some women find it more difficult to sing in their soprano voice after they have been belting.

SURPRISES

You may not know how many people you'll find behind the table when you walk in. You may not have expected the room to be only ten feet by ten feet, or to be a barn-like forty feet square. If these things could potentially throw you off, ask the door monitor how many people are behind the table, and try to peek into the room as someone exits. Factors and curves that you can't control will always be thrown at you, but being prepared and flexible are qualities that you can and must rely on.

CHAPTER 7

During the Audition

I like to compare your first few experiences in the audition room to the first few times you drive a car. At first you are almost too focused, very nervous, and tense. After a few weeks, you can drive with one hand, look at the road, check the rearview mirror, and take in all the lovely sights around you.

Although no cut-and-dried rules define the auditioning process, there is an understood industry "norm." This chapter will discuss the unspoken dos and don'ts as it takes you through the process, step-by-step.

FOLLOW INSTRUCTIONS

When you are called to enter the audition room, pay attention to the door monitor's actions. Is this person taking your headshot-résumé into the audition room, or will you deliver it to the panel yourself? Will he or she announce your name, or do you need to introduce yourself?

It is not advisable to approach the audition table and shake everyone's hands. It takes too much time, and the auditors usually do not want to be bothered. The basic rule is that if an auditor offers his or her hand, then of course you should reciprocate.

If your name is not announced when you are brought in, say your name before you start to sing. (You do not need to offer the name of the song or its authors, unless asked.) This will ensure that the panel is reading your résumé and not someone else's by mistake. Don't assume the procedure will be the same at every audition. Look at and listen to what is going on around you.

PERSONAL BELONGINGS

Always bring your personal belongings into the room with you. Unfortunately, leaving your Walkman, scarf, or new songbook in the holding area can be very tempting to a starving actor. Set your things down right by the inside of the door or next to the piano, so you can easily grab them when you are through. Have your music book in one hand, ready to go, so you don't need to search for it.

ACCOMPANIST

Assuming the monitor has given the casting people your headshot, go directly to the pianist first. Give this person your music as quickly and as politely as possible.

When you are talking to the pianist, stand upstage of the piano so your rear end isn't sticking out at the panel. You should spend no more than ten seconds explaining your music to the pianist. If it takes longer, then your music probably isn't prepared properly with the correct markings.

Many pianists, including myself, are insulted when you explain your song tempo by snapping your fingers at them. Sing or speak a phrase of the song to demonstrate the tempo. If you need to, close your eyes and set the tempo and mood as if you were performing it; otherwise, because you're nervous, you might give a faster tempo than you mean to.

Try giving the pianist the pulse or groove of the song instead of just the melody, as this really helps explain the tempo. Does the song have a soft-shoe feel, a swing feel, a jazz-waltz feel, or what?

The very first section of many songs often begins with a "verse" that has no actual tempo. The singer has the freedom to sing the musical phrases freely, almost like a sung conversation. This section is often notated in the music as either "rubato," "ad-lib," or "conversationally." Therefore, when you approach the pianist in your audition, you only need to give him or her the tempo where the tempo begins—usually notated as the "refrain" or "chorus."

On your way to the pianist, you may certainly say, "Hello," or, "Good morning," to the panelists, but don't assume or expect a response. They may still be busy talking or writing about the person before you, so don't take their silence personally.

USING FURNITURE OR PROPS

Using a chair at a sixteen-bar chorus call is not recommended. Unless you can truly justify a need for it (such as your character's being handicapped), don't waste your time. Honestly, sixteen bars really don't give you enough time dramatically to earn the need to stand up or sit down. The audition is not about your use of props and furniture.

For that matter, you should never assume to *find* a chair at a non-union audition. (Equity does require a chair for actors in the audition room.)

ON YOUR MARK, GET SET, GO?

When you have finished explaining your music to the pianist, walk to the center of the room and wait until you are acknowledged by one of the casting people before you begin. Give yourself some distance from the panelists—positioning yourself about six feet away from them is good. They need to see the "whole picture"—plus a lot of auditors are made very uncomfortable when performers stand too close.

The auditors will either nod to you or simply say, "Whenever you're ready." It is not necessary to announce the name of your song. If someone asks you afterward, then this person is the one taking the initiative in taking the time to converse with you.

Reminder: do not start singing while the auditors are still discussing someone else or writing out their lunch order. You deserve the panel's complete attention. If, however, they start talking or eating while you are singing, you must ignore it, because there is nothing you can do. Don't waste your time or lose your concentration by trying to second-guess what they are talking about—partly because it's probably not about you.

CAN YOU LOOK AT THEM?

Should you focus on the panel during your audition? Individual casting directors, directors, musical directors, choreographers, and producers all respond to this matter differently. Most musical theater auditors endorse the following.

Do not sing a ballad directly to an auditor. Singing a love song, for example, to a particular panel member may create an awkward and uncomfortable situation that can very easily be misinterpreted. Instead, choose a spot in the vicinity of the panel. As you start to audition a lot, you will learn that some auditors never want to be sung to.

Once I became involved in an incredibly awkward situation. A woman sang "If I Loved You," and decided to perform it directly to me. She *never* moved her focus away. I was so tense and nervous as I realized I became a part of her scene. I started to blush and before I knew it, my left leg was shaking up and down so fast that my bottle of water fell off the table while she was still singing. I was so happy the noise created enough of a distraction for me to turn away and not look up again.

You can control the responses of an imaginary scene partner, but you can't even predict those of an auditor. Put yourself in the place of a panelist: he or she is there to focus objectively on *your* work. If you make this person your scene partner, you're suddenly demanding that he or she enter the scene, and respond to your character *in* character. You're expecting the panelist to be an actor in a song he or she may not even know. How carefully and objectively can this person concentrate on your performance under these circumstances?

Exception noted: when singing your up-tempo, feel free to include the panel from time to time. If your selection is a presentational song such as " I Feel a Song Comin' On," or "Lullaby of Broadway," you should allow your eyes to bounce off the panel as if you were giving a lecture. Include everyone in your range of focus, but never stay focused on one person. Personally, I think it looks odd to completely ignore the fact that five or six living, breathing people are sitting ten feet in front of you while singing such lyrics as "Come on along and listen to / the lullaby of Broadway" (from the musical *42nd Street*).

LOCATING YOUR IMAGINARY SCENE PARTNER

If your character is singing to someone specific in his or her life, place your imaginary scene partner either one head's length above the panel or choose a space between two panel members. This will allow them to see your face and yet not feel intruded upon.

EXTREME FOCUSES

Be careful not to choose focuses that shut out the panel. For example, if you are singing to an imaginary baby, don't put her one foot in front of you. In that case you will be forced to look down, directing your energy to the floor, instead of out to the panel. Put the baby or the crib between two panel members, or just to the right or left of the panel, to keep your performance out front. The same applies when you are singing to God or to the heavens. Don't place your focus directly straight up. Put God behind, and just above the panelists, so they can still see your face.

Always remind yourself that the auditors are sitting there to perform a task. They should be able to jot down notes or confer with each other when necessary. They cannot and do not want to participate in your presentation. This is an audition, not a paid performance earning a response with applause. You will need to get used to hearing silence when you are through singing and acting. Remember, the panel is there to observe, to ask any necessary questions, and to take copious notes on your presentation. This is not to infer that if you are funny, they won't laugh.

You want the auditors to take the journey with you, without their being a part of your journey.

TAKING DIRECTION

Having someone on the panel ask you to make adjustments or request to hear other songs or monologues isn't something to panic about. Most of the time it means that an auditor is interested in you but needs to find out more about you— for example, what are the different colors of your voice, are you directable, do you understand and speak the language (theater) of the director, or do you have a interesting personality?

Listen carefully to what the director or musical director is looking for. If you are asked something that you either do not understand or cannot do, be honest and say so. It is perfectly fine to ask if there is something else you can show that might alleviate any concerns he or she may have.

For example, if the musical director wants to hear a song in a higher range and you don't have one, ask the pianist if one of the songs in your binder can be transposed. If the director wants to see your comic abilities and you don't have a funny song, ask if you may sing one of your serious songs with a humorous twist.

"SIDES" AND "COLD READINGS"

"Sides" are monologues or scenes from the script of the show that you are auditioning for. They enable the director to hear you read the role you are being considered for, using this excerpt from the play. Sometimes the director may want you to do a "cold reading," which means you have about ten minutes to look over a scene before you present it to the auditors. If so, take the "sides" out into the hallway and read them carefully. You may ask the director if there's anything specific you should know ahead of time, although usually he or she wants to hear your take and interpretation first.

If you have been given sides at Monday's audition and are asked to come back on Thursday to read them, you must be prepared to do so. Do note that casting people very rarely, if ever, ask that sides be memorized. One of the problems of presenting completely memorized sides is that doing so unconsciously raises the auditor's expectations; your audition might be viewed as a (poorly) finished performance. Also, memorizing puts an extra burden on you and deflects your concentration from interpretation of the role.

Make acting choices—whether right or wrong, make choices. Try to identify the writing style and tone of the scene. Is it comical, presentational, classical, satirical, or. . .? If there is time and interest, the director will take a few moments to give you some adjustments after your first reading, and have you try it again to see how well you take direction.

STANDING OUT

Your goal is to distinguish yourself from every other person auditioning. Assuming that everyone who showed up has a nice voice, a good look, a neat résumé, and a pleasant personality, what can possibly make you stand out? Here comes my profound answer: the ability to be you. I know—easier said than done. This requires the nerve to open up your heart and soul to strangers. The freedom and ability to communicate your unique inner thoughts and feelings to a panel or audience of complete strangers is what will separate you from everyone else. It's what makes you interesting to watch and to listen to. It is what makes you human. It is what enables the panel or audience to connect with and relate to you as a singular person placed in an imaginary circumstance. Otherwise, you become a faceless body singing loud, high notes and projecting no real sense of an individual with any point of view. In other words, you become one more photo in the circular file.

Here is a good example of "being yourself": in 1992, I was asked to audition for the pianist for *The Fantasticks*. (The only instruments in the show were a piano and a harp.) I was told ahead of time what to prepare and that the audition would take place at New York City's Sullivan Street Playhouse, on the actual stage where the production was playing.

I arrived there early enough to thaw out my hands from the cold weather and to relax (as much as I could). I heard a few pianists ahead of me playing and I immediately freaked out; they were such great players. At that point, I wanted to get up and leave, but suddenly they announced my name and brought me onto the stage. Here comes the fun part: I would be playing for composer Harvey Schmidt!!! He told me he would sing the songs while I accompanied him on the piano. Whoa!!! Talk about being nervous.

My hands were so sweaty from nerves that they kept on sliding off the keys. I know that I definitely played some wrong notes during the audition, but there was nothing I could do about it except try to focus.

The audition was finally over and Mr. Schmidt couldn't have been more complimentary, though I felt like crap. Later that evening I got a phone call offering me the job. I was honestly stunned. I did something one should never do. I asked why I was hired. I was told that my ability to follow a singer, my sense of musicality, and the heart and soul I put into my playing won them over immediately. They weren't so concerned about a few wrong notes. They knew I would be trained and would ultimately learn the score properly. Wow! Just being me was enough to get the job.

WHEN YOU ARE THROUGH

When you've finished singing your song, stand and wait quietly for further instructions. The panelists may ask to hear another song, or they may whisper back and forth for a moment, or they may simply look up at you and say, "Thank you for coming in today; that's all we need right now." Not needing to see or hear anything more is not necessarily a bad thing. As I stated earlier, it means, for better or for worse, that they have heard and seen what they need to *at this time.*

It is strongly advisable *not* to ask the auditors when they will be making casting decisions. More importantly, do not start offering them all of the other songs you've prepared. Say, "Thank you," then thank the pianist and exit the room. If you have questions regarding the casting process, you can certainly ask the door monitor. The monitor is hired to help keep the audition running smoothly and orderly. This person is the one who usually brings you into the room and sometimes even announces your name to the panel. Hopefully, the casting director or producer has given him or her answers to questions like "Do you know when they'll be making their final casting choices?" or "If I get cast, do you know when the rehearsals will start?"

The reality of the casting process differs with each theater. Some may tell you on the spot that they want to see you for a callback, while others may not contact you for several weeks (if they do want to see you again).

Many actors leave the room with a defeated, self-pitying look on their faces. This is a mistake. Be aware that your body language tells the panel more than you can ever imagine. The minute the auditors sense someone with attitude, for instance,

You may not see *it*, but we do!

that person's headshot will likely be moved from the "callback" pile to the "no" pile. You should always exit the audition room professionally—meaning you should save your comments and your opinions (spoken and unspoken) regarding how well you did or didn't do, till after you've left the room.

I'll never forget the time a young lady turned to us (the panel) before exiting the room and asked us why we didn't want to hear her sing another song. We were all stunned. Nobody wanted to hurt her feelings, so the director told her we were running behind and we had heard what we needed to for now. She still wouldn't accept that as a good enough reason. She complained that she had waited three hours to finally come in the room to sing and she deserved to sing both of her prepared songs. Finally, I stood up and told her that we didn't want to hear another song because we were not interested in her. She then asked me why.

At that point I asked the door monitor to please escort her out. The truth is, we had been interested in calling her back without hearing another song, but now her pushiness and rudeness turned us off from wanting to work with her.

CHAPTER 8

After the Audition

You will rarely (if ever) receive feedback from your audition. You must learn to sense for yourself how well you did. If you feel you did well, allow yourself to feel good about it. I hate to shock you with this, but getting the job should only be half of your goal. As I mentioned earlier, what's really important is being seen by as many directors and casting directors as possible, to begin your networking process.

Learn from each audition what worked for you and what didn't work for you, and why. With nerves and adrenaline flowing, was your vocal range not what you thought it was? Were you able to follow through on what you prepared? If not, why? Were your instructions to the pianist unclear? Did someone on the panel throw you off by yawning? Did a loud fire engine drive by while you were singing?

Once you identify what distracts you, find a way to rise above it for your next audition.

CALLBACKS

If you have sparked the panel's interest and are called back immediately after your audition, before you leave, check with the monitor about any details regarding the callback—such as what to sing and what time the auditors want you there. The panel may also tell you in the audition room that they want to call you back, and that the monitor or an assistant will telephone you later with the specifics.

Remember what you sang and what you wore at your first audition. If you're called back, sing the same song—unless directed otherwise—and wear the same outfit. This will help the casting people recognize you. They may have seen hundreds of performers on that first day, so giving them a visual and aural reminder of who you are and why you were called back gives you an advantage. Conversely, if at the original audition, you came in with your hair down, wearing a blue dress, and singing a ballad, then returned to the callback with your hair up, in a red dress, and singing an uptempo, the panel will think they are seeing you for the first time.

It is not necessary to sing the same song or to wear the same outfit at a second callback.

KEEP A LOG

Cut the casting notice out of *Back Stage*, etc., or download it from its Web site and print it out. Then either tape it to a journal or in your appointment book. After the audition, write down who was on the panel, what you sang, what you wore, and how you think it went. Keep this information for the next time you audition for the same casting person.

FOLLOW UP

After an audition is over, is it normal to follow up with a thank-you note to the producer and/or director? In a chorus-call situation, where you do not know anyone on the panel, a thank-you card would be silly. A producer would probably wonder, "Who is this?" and then throw your card in the garbage. If you have worked for this director or producer before, however, then a thank-you may be appropriate, but still not at all necessary.

If a particular casting director has called you in for the first time or has called you in often to audition (and therefore knows who you are), then perhaps a card saying, "It was great to see you again, and good luck with your upcoming season," or, "Once again, thanks for calling me in," would certainly be appreciated and appropriate. I do think that self-promotion disguised as a holiday card is tacky.

If you do choose to send a card or a note, don't wait more than a few days to mail it. The casting director may see hundreds of other actors, for more than one project, in the course of only a week. Your card will more effectively remind him or her of you and your audition if it is received soon after you've been seen in person.

My philosophy is that you need the folks behind the table as much as they need you. You need them for the work, and they need you in their show. Remember that you are the one who got all dressed up, took off from work, and spent money on a coach. I believe, therefore, that the auditors have just as much reason to thank you as you do them.

NO SECOND-GUESSING

You have no control over how many people are being hired. You have no control over a terrible pianist. If the show being cast is *West Side Story*, you have no idea that perhaps the producer has already hired an actor from his hometown to play Tony, and that actor is only 5'6". You may have given the perfect audition, but you are a 5'8" Maria. All you may hear is, "Thank you," and you can't figure out why you didn't get called back. Don't drive yourself crazy trying to read into the auditors' responses (or lack thereof) during your audition. That is certainly not where your focus should be! Furthermore, don't waste your energy after the audition by trying to figure out why you didn't get a callback. Many factors go into making these casting decisions, and too many of them are beyond your control.

THE ROLE IS ALREADY CAST

I have often been hired to direct a show musically in which some of the principal roles and ensemble parts have already been cast by the producer or the director ahead of time. This is another situation in which you won't be called back for a part that you're really right for. It is not fair, but it is reality. Many directors offer a role to an actor they have worked with before, or sometimes using a local actor saves a producer housing and transportation costs. (Remember show *business*?)

Auditions for the precast role will still take place, in case the actor already hired drops out at the last minute. At least the director will have seen other people who can replace him or her if necessary.

WHOM SHOULD YOU BE?

I used to try to figure out what a producer and director wanted my personality to be like. I'd always heard that directors like to work with nice, collaborative people, so for one full year I would show up at all of my interviews with a very friendly persona. Oddly enough, I wasn't getting hired. I learned later on that they felt they didn't see any leadership qualities in me because I was so nice and friendly. I thought about it and understood their position on that issue. I agreed that as a musical director and conductor, I needed to display the serious, authoritative qualities that they were looking for. So I began to bring these into my auditions. To my dismay, I still was not being hired. This time the producers and directors were leery because they felt I was a too-serious musician. They thought I lacked the people skills that working with singers and an orchestra require.

Eventually I took the approach of not worrying about how to "present" myself. I had to trust my real personality as well as my musical abilities. It finally occurred to me that my employers shouldn't be surprised by who I really am two months later when I arrive on the job. They should see and know who I am now. If they don't like it, then it's better for them and for me to know this up front.

When I was able to integrate this philosophy into my life, interviews became less stressful, and my success rate went up seventy-five percent. I needed to figure this out through trial and error, as you do. The safest, easiest, and most effective approach is to be you.

CHAPTER 9

The Pianist

The audition pianist plays a very important role in the audition room. In many ways, he or she can make or break the success of your audition. Of course, it's unfair that you have prepared very hard for an audition, but that the person playing for you is a complete stranger who has never rehearsed with you before. Still, you can definitely take many precautions to prevent a problem.

COMMON COURTESY

Be courteous to the pianist, as this person has been sitting there playing the piano all day. Keep in mind that the pianist may be affiliated with the theater, so if you are rude, he or she will tell the panel as soon as you exit the room to stick your headshot in the "no" pile. The accompanist may also be the assistant musical director, and therefore part of the casting process. Or the pianist may be someone who plays for lots of auditions that you surely will be attending. Stay positive even if the pianist is dreadful. A lot of them are young and getting experience in the same way that you are (not that this excuses their incompetence).

PROPER KEYS

Remember you should not be asking audition pianists to sight-read from hand-written sloppy scores, or to transpose (change keys) on sight. What *is* acceptable for transposed music?

1. The ideal is to have your song transposed on a computer. The current rate in New York City ranges from ten to fifteen dollars per page. Having your music transposed on a computer is like having the song written and published for you. The music includes *your* key, *your* markings, and a proper musical introduction and ending that you've rehearsed and chosen to use.

   Most vocal coaches have the ability and resources to transpose your music to your proper key on their computers. If your coach does not, ask for any names of people who can, or ask other actors whom they use to transpose their music. You can also look in trade publications like *Back Stage* for people who advertise their services for transposing music.

2. The next option is to have your music rewritten neatly by a music copyist. Long before personal computers, people actually got paid to handwrite music, and many still are.

3. If your song is a very popular known standard such as "I Got Rhythm," then chord symbols written in the music are probably okay, although you never know who is playing and what his or her transposition skills are.

Ignoring these three options could lead to a disastrous audition. Remember, the pianist already has a job for the day; *you* are the one hoping to get work. Bringing in sloppy music is preventable.

TEMPO AND STYLE

Although humming or singing the melody of your song is certainly an acceptable means of communicating your tempo to the pianist, also naming the musical style will more clearly describe that tempo. Becoming familiar with musical styles such as swing, jazz, waltz, soft-shoe, cakewalk, pop ballad, tango, gospel, march, beguine, funk, etc., can often help you dictate the tempo and feel to the pianist. If you are not aware of the style of your song, sing the melody while demonstrating the pulse of the beat with your hand (not by snapping your fingers).

CUE THE PIANIST

Communicate to the pianist when you want him or her to begin playing the musical introduction. Too often the pianist starts to play before you are ready to sing, because at a busy audition, the auditors want to keep up the pace. As an audition pianist, I was always told, "Keep things moving. We want to see everyone— get 'em in and get 'em out." Let the pianist know specifically what kind of a cue you are going to provide. It could be as simple as "When I lift my head" or "When I nod to you." If you just stand there, most pianists are programmed to start playing.

Now, if the pianist doesn't wait for you, it is up to you to take control of the situation. Either stop and say that you weren't ready and kindly remind him or her of the cue, or continue singing (if you feel the abrupt start hasn't ruined your concentration).

WHAT IF THE PIANIST IS RUINING YOUR SONG?

At a sixteen-bar chorus call, there is not a lot you can do to correct a pianist who is playing poorly. If something goes wrong within the first two measures of the song, such as a wrong tempo or feel, then stop immediately. Do not ask the auditors if you can start over again, because you are giving them an opening to answer, "No." Simply stop and say, "I think I gave the pianist the wrong tempo." Walk to the pianist and provide the correct tempo, quickly (even if you already gave him or her the correct tempo the first time). This shows the panel that you are taking charge and staying in control of the situation.

TOO LATE TO START OVER

Once you are halfway through your sixteen bars, and you know something is wrong with the pianist, it is really too late to stop and start over. If the pianist is truly incompetent, the panel will know. If you spend the entire time rolling your eyes at the pianist while you are singing, everything you have prepared to show the panel at this audition will have been lost. (Besides which, this kind of behavior on your part would be extremely unprofessional.)

At an agent-submission audition for which you have an appointment, time is a bit more flexible for stopping to sing and talk with the pianist. Again, blame the error on yourself and remedy the problem. If you sense that the pianist isn't very good or experienced, you might want to find a different song to sing—one that has an easier piano accompaniment or that is more familiar. Rather than asking the pianist if he or she can play the song, I suggest asking whether if he or she knows this song, so you are not hurting anyone's feelings.

BRINGING YOUR OWN PIANIST

Should you bring your own pianist to an audition? For a sixteen-bar chorus call, there should be no reason to do so. If your sixteen bars are so difficult to sight-read, then you have probably chosen the wrong song to sing. Bringing your own pianist will also cost you time and money for rehearsing ahead of time and playing at the actual audition.

However, when an important audition comes up and the casting notice requests a full song, you may want to consider bringing your own accompanist if the most appropriate song you have for this audition is very difficult. Do not worry that the audition pianist will be insulted if you walk in with your own accompanist. I'm sure he or she will welcome the break.

If you have a callback for a Broadway show and composer-lyricist Stephen Sondheim will be present, you may feel more comfortable with your own pianist playing for you. (I am not insinuating that audition pianists at the Broadway level aren't extremely competent.)

CHAPTER 10

Vocal Training

VOCAL COACH VERSUS VOICE TEACHER

Which one do you need to have and what are the differences? A voice teacher is different than a vocal coach in that a teacher primarily focuses on vocal technique. A coach investigates the lyrics and music from an acting standpoint while preparing your overall presentation for an audition.

Depending on your financial situation and vocal needs, you may want to study with a voice teacher instead of, or in addition to, a vocal coach.

VOCAL COACH

Okay, you're on your own searching for audition material and you realize that you need some guidance. Or maybe you've found an interesting song, but you need someone to teach it to you and to prepare it musically to see if it really is right for your voice. What are you going to do? You are going to find a vocal coach.

A good experienced vocal coach is one who can show your voice and personality at their best, by helping you find and choose the right material. A good coach serves as an objective eye and ear that can offer comments and give constructive criticism in putting together the best overall package for your audition.

How Do You Find a Good Coach?

As you start to audition and work, you will meet actors and singers who can recommend a coach to you. Once you start performing in shows, you will work with musical directors whom you might enjoy coaching with, or who can at least recommend someone else to you.

Many coaches are listed in *Back Stage* and on Playbill.com, for instance, but whenever possible you should try to get a referral from someone whose work you respect. When in doubt, good word-of-mouth is the way to go.

What Is the Going Rate?

As this book goes to press (2005), the rate in New York City is somewhere in between thirty-five and sixty-five dollars an hour, depending on the coach's experience and reputation. A young coach, recently out of college, would probably charge less, to build up a clientele and to gain experience.

Music and Lyrics

I notice that too many coaches find music for their clients based solely on those clients' vocal capabilities, but this is just half the battle. Your songs need to fit your personality and look as well.

As far as I'm concerned, auditioning with a song that suits your voice is a given. The real issue is, what is going to make you stand out? What song will allow you to be interesting? How well can you connect and relate to the lyrics and the subject matter? Too many coaches and singers don't take these factors into consideration.

With so many songs to pick from, how can you and your coach narrow down the endless choices?

Let me explain my approach as a vocal coach:

1. When a singer first contacts me, I explain my coaching method on the phone before we discuss anything further. Once the singer and I have made it past the first conversation, I set up a thirty-minute session in which I chat with the singer to get a sense of who he or she is. I ask how this singer perceives him- or herself: romantic lead, character actress, comedienne, etc. Then, I look at the résumé to see what experience he or she has, as well as how other directors and musical directors have cast this person in the past. (Not that I have to agree with them.)

2. I ask what types of roles and shows the singer would see him- or herself doing, as well as what kinds this person would never consider, based on his or her interests.

3. Finally, I have this person sing a few songs for me that contrast in musical style and dramatic content. Based on what I hear and see, I will normally pull around twenty-five songs. When all is said and done, if this singer winds up loving and keeping six to eight, then I consider myself successful.

How Do You Want the Panelists to See You?

Remember that the casting people can only form an opinion of you based on what you choose to show them. You must keep in mind that you are your own product—a commodity that you are trying to sell, just like a box of laundry detergent. You must clearly understand what you do well today, at this stage of your life; and you must clearly know why we should be interested in you.

For example, a consumer who wants to clean his or her clothes goes looking for laundry detergent; this person is not shopping for dish soap or furniture polish. The decision to purchase a specific detergent is based on the information provided: packaging, price, effectiveness, scent.

If you are a "character" type, yet choose to sing a leading lady song and dress in jeans, then you are pulling the focus away from yourself and sending mixed messages. However talented you may be, the panelists don't know what to do with you because you haven't helped them define you and your type. (You're a laundry detergent labeled "dish soap.") They'll put you in the "maybe" pile. The maybe pile consists of a bunch of actors whom they cannot decide whether to call back. Unfortunately, by the end of the day that pile is usually discarded because enough talented, distinct types have come in.

If you are more than one type, then I encourage you to audition for everything you are right for. However, you must choose material appropriate to the role you would like to be considered for, so there is no question as to what you are there for.

Using Your Session Wisely

You may run into a situation where you only need a coach to record some songs on a tape for you to practice with. If that's the case, make clear at the outset that you are not looking for a coaching, but a taping. Some coaches, like me, aren't interested in only making tapes for singers. I personally find it frustrating to make tapes without commenting on the songs and giving suggestions.

Assuming your coach is happy to record songs for you, make sure you are somewhat familiar with the style of the songs as far as tempos go, so you don't leave complaining that all of the songs were recorded too fast.

Have your cassette tape cued up and ready to record. Too many singers spend too much time rewinding their tapes, looking for a good place to start recording. When you are ready, do a quick check to make sure that the volume is up and you pushed "record." Again, it's your time and money.

Coaches prefer clients who are responsible and know what they want to accomplish in their sessions.

A well-known actress hired me for two hours to put some music on tape for her. We went page by page by page by page for almost three hours. She wanted each song recorded twice: once with the melody only, and once with the piano accompaniment only. At the end of the session, she went to take the tape out of the tape player and realized she had had the "pause" button on the entire time. Nothing was recorded. I felt bad, but I still charged her for my time.

Types of Coaches

There are many different types of coaches, each having different strengths and weaknesses. In choosing a vocal coach it is important to find out about his or her approach to a song, dramatically and musically. I approach the lyric as a monologue. For me and the singer that usually determines when and where to breathe, and where the climax is, as well as most of the dynamics. Certain coaches may not be skilled in "monologing" the lyrics, or even be interested in it. Their strength may lie in arranging music, transposing music, and helping you choose material, but not in addressing the acting aspect of a song. Don't forget that in a theater audition you are looking for material that shows off your vocal and acting abilities.

You must figure out what areas you need the most help with. Ask yourself what strengths in a coach are the most important for you right now.

VOICE TEACHER

In choosing a voice teacher I suggest that you allow three lessons to determine whether or not this person is right for you. I think it takes that long to see whether a teacher's approach works for you.

Things to look for in selecting a voice teacher

The following checklist will help you select the voice teacher best suited for you:

1. Does this teacher play the piano?

2. Do you need to bring an accompanist?

3. If so, who pays for the accompanist?

4. What type of vocalizations are students given?

5. Does this teacher hold master classes so you can hear his or her other students?

6. Who are some past and present students?

7. What is this teacher's educational and professional background?

8. Will this teacher, and can he or she, work on theater repertoire as opposed to only classical literature?

9. Does this teacher travel out of town frequently to perform?

10. What methods are used—mirrors, imagery, etc.?

11. Can you pay by check, or cash only?

I firmly believe that you need to grasp your teacher's technique and process well enough to make them work for you when you're working alone. A good teacher is one who enables you to understand what is being taught.

If you are on the road for six months performing, you need to be able to care for your voice and warm up properly without having your voice teacher present. It's not a bad idea to ask your teacher to record some of the vocalizations on tape that you use in your lessons, so you can warm up.

Ideally, your understanding of the technique should be so clear that you could teach it to someone else. When a singer only sings well during voice lessons, it usually indicates that he or she really doesn't know what he or she is doing right. Learn to sing correctly on purpose, not accidentally.

Going Rate

As this book goes to press, the rate in New York City can range anywhere from fifty to one hundred dollars for a forty-five minute lesson. Teachers who only accept clients who are at a highly successful level probably charge a lot more.

Source for Music?

Don't necessarily rely on your voice teacher to be a leading force in finding musical theater songs, because the majority of voice teachers' backgrounds are in "classical" music.

Are You Good Enough for the Teacher?

Do you have to audition to be in this person's studio? If so, realize that this teacher may only take singers who have already reached a certain level of proficiency. Conversely, he or she might only teach beginners, either by choice or due to his or her own level of experience.

Young Teachers

Many recent college graduates who are beginning their singing and teaching careers probably charge very reasonable rates. Check local colleges and universities to find out about recent graduates they might be able to recommend you to. Postgraduate students tend to be more available, more patient, more enthusiastic, and less jaded than older teachers.

OTHER FACTORS FOR COACHES AND TEACHERS

Cancellation

What is the voice teacher's or coach's cancellation policy, and are there any exceptions? Most of the time you are required to give twenty-four hours' notice to cancel, meaning if you cancel on the morning of your lesson you still have to pay for it. Certainly, if this is the teacher's main source of income, you must respect his policy.

As a coach, the one exception I allow for a last-minute cancellation is a callback that your agent just scheduled for tomorrow because the casting director can't see you at any other time. Your ultimate aim is to get the job. If my coaching contributes to your getting the callback for the job, why would I not be supportive by allowing you to make up your lesson at another time?

Availability

Is your voice teacher or coach heavily booked all the time by other clients? How flexible is his or her schedule from week to week? If an important audition came up, could you be scheduled in at the last minute, or is advance notice always required?

PERSONAL VOCAL CARE

The voice is a unique instrument in that it is physically a part of your body. Unlike a clarinetist, for instance, you can't put your instrument away in a case when you've finished performing. Any tension, abuse, or fatigue that you might cause to your body will have a major effect on your voice. You must learn to respect and care for your voice so you can always rely on it. Water and rest are the best medicine for your voice. If you are stuck in a dry hotel room or dressing room, you may want to invest in a portable steamer to help prevent your throat from drying out.

If you are playing the leading role in a musical, and you have to perform eight times a week, you must learn the limitations of your voice. It might mean not socializing after the show every night, or not talking on the phone for hours every day. If you are on tour, traveling on a bus daily, you must be careful not to shout across the bus to your friends or you will develop a sore throat. You are being paid to perform a service each night; therefore, you must be responsible.

As a pianist/conductor, I do not allow myself to participate in activities such as bowling and rollerblading, because I can't afford to sprain my wrists or break my arm while under contract to play or conduct.

SUMMING UP

What works for someone else may not necessarily work for you. If you find a wonderful voice teacher or coach whom you dislike personally, or who makes you feel uncomfortable, you may want to reassess the situation to decide which influences you more: his or her talent or an intimidating, unfriendly approach.

I am not implying that your teacher or coach should only be kind and understanding, and give you cookies. Vocal training should be a growing, stretching, and stimulating experience. If it's too pleasant and comfortable, there's a good chance you probably aren't learning anything new.

Only you can know under what conditions you gain the most. Learn to trust your instincts.

CHAPTER 11

Dance Training

Dance is a major part of the musical theater genre. Too many talented actors and singers can't book a job because they lack the necessary skills, or because they simply lack the confidence. The only way to get better and more confident is by taking dance classes.

Every musical-theater performer should be in dance class every week as part of his or her routine. Even if you think you are a leading-man or -woman type, you should learn to "move well" proficiently. Many leading men and women assume that the ensemble will do all the dancing around them. That may often be the case, but the better the leads can dance, the more the choreographer can do with a number.

Legendary Tony Award–winning dancers such as Donna McKechnie, Karen Ziemba, Ann Reinking, Chita Rivera, and Liza Minelli still take dance classes as part of their weekly routines, to stay in shape and to hone their dancing skills.

WHAT TYPE OF DANCE?

Not all dancers must be extremely proficient in *every* area of dance—some may be brilliant tappers, while others may excel in ballet. To know how to do all of them at a moderate level is what's important. If you are a trained jazz and modern dancer, you should be studying tap. You may never have aspirations to be in a tap-heavy show like *42nd Street*, but many shows do incorporate different dance styles, so the more versatile you are, the more marketable you will become.

STYLE

What are the different schools of dance? How does Agnes de Mille differ from Bob Fosse? How does Jerome Robbins differ from Michael Bennett? In what ways do they use the body differently? What body type best suits a specific choreographer's style? Susan Stroman and Tommy Tune, for example, tend to hire tall, slim dancers between 5'8" and 6'2".

Dancing isn't just about entertaining an audience; it is about telling a story. In musical theater it further expresses a character's emotion or need—an emotion or need that cannot be told through dialogue or song alone; it *must* be danced.

To broaden your sense of style—aside from studying these different choreographers' work in a dance class—try watching old movie musicals to see the different approaches created and developed by individual choreographers. Among the great

You should hear me sing!

movies to start with are *Singin' in the Rain*, *Brigadoon*, *West Side Story*, *Summer Stock*, and *Sweet Charity*.

You can also learn a lot about dance styles from carefully watching and observing great dancers—such as Fred Astaire, Gene Kelly, Shirley MacLaine, Ann Miller, and Gower Champion, to name a few—in films.

I like to compare dancers to pianists. Pianists study technique to build strong, agile hands, just as dancers study technique to build their bodies. When I arrived in New York City, I learned quickly, however, that technique was just a part of landing a job. "Style" was the important word. Could I approach composers like Kern, Porter, Gershwin, Rodgers, Loesser, Strouse, Schwartz, Coleman, Lloyd Webber, and Sondheim with stylistic correctness? Luckily, I could. Many other pianists with amazing technique never booked the jobs that I got because they lacked an understanding of style. As I mentioned earlier, style is learned and absorbed by constantly reading, practicing, watching, listening, and doing.

SUGGESTED ATTIRE FOR A DANCE AUDITION (MEN AND WOMEN)

The following suggestions regarding attire for a dance audition will help you "look the part" of a dancer:

1. Stay away from wearing several layers of clothing. Choreographers tend not to like to see dance clothes covered up by shorts and sweatshirts, because they are looking at your figure and body shape. Wearing layers also screams, "I'm not a dancer!"

2. When in doubt, wear character or jazz shoes, unless directed otherwise; have tap shoes with you, just in case.

3. Dance attire can be any color.

4. Women should wear makeup and keep their hair up or pulled back so it doesn't bounce around or cover the face.

5. A bandanna or headband is great to use if you have long hair that needs to be pulled back.

AT A DANCE CALL

Many other people will be learning the combination with you. Pay close attention to the choreographer's instructions. Try not to let yourself become overwhelmed by fancy moves. Break the combination down into sections for yourself. The mind tends to absorb more information faster when you can focus on one aspect at a time. For instance, learn the steps first, then add the arms—and please feel free to ask the choreographer questions.

The choreographer wants to see you having fun while performing the combination with commitment. He or she is looking to get a sense of your personality as well as your technique. Do you exude lots of energy, or are you petrified and concentrating only on the steps? Are you about technique alone, without artistry?

Even if you can't learn all the steps, "trick" the choreographer by the way you sell your performance in your face and body language. If you know you missed a few steps, keep on doing the number to show that you are interesting to watch onstage.

If you choose to attend an audition, don't waste your time beating yourself up about your lack of dance confidence and/or experience. Try to enjoy yourself and view a dance call as a free dance class.

DON'T STOP HERE

Having read Part One, you should now have a clear understanding of what auditioning for musicals entails. But to limit your career by seeing yourself only as a musical theater performer is needless. In my opinion, acting is acting! Yes, there are different styles of acting, but a trained actor is still a trained actor. Being open to doing both musicals and straight plays also expands your opportunities for work. Part Two will show you how to make the crossover. It focuses on acting auditions— on how to find, rehearse, and deliver the "right" monologues. I think you will be pleasantly surprised at the similar approaches to preparing for musicals and straight plays.

PART TWO

Acting Monologues

CHAPTER 12

Introduction: The Monologue Process

"Okay, now let's see your monologue."

Those words can send your nervous system into overdrive. But auditioning with a monologue doesn't have to be a fearful mystery—and it won't be after you've read this section's step-by-step explanation of how to find, rehearse, and perform your monologues.

After working with hundreds of students and fellow actors in monologue workshops, classes, and one-on-one coaching over the years, I began thinking about why people were so frustrated with the whole auditioning process. I came up with this: they had no plan. They didn't have the proper skills with which to begin the process. Or they weren't even aware that there *was* a process—a structured path toward finding that perfect monologue for an audition, that special piece that, performed by you, will make the casting director look up from your résumé, put down his or her coffee cup, and want to see more!

MONOLOGUES ARE ESSENTIAL

When my acting students are ready to begin the audition process, they go to professional photographers to have their pictures taken. Then they ask me to look at the contact sheets from their photo sessions. They approach me with sixty to 200 tiny pictures, all with the same concern: finding just the right shot. They have spent weeks or months seeking out the best photographers, choosing their most flattering outfits, and even hiring hairstylists and makeup artists for their photo shoots. Each student wants to know which little image on his or her contact sheets will get a job.

"Before I see your contact sheet," I answer, "how about we look at your monologue choices?" There is silence and a blank stare. "You do have monologues picked out, right? Do you have as many monologues to choose from as you do pictures?" Again, there is an awkward silence. Finally, the answer comes: "Not yet, but I'll find something."

Something? You'll find *something*? I am amazed at how many actors spend hours examining their picture choices, worrying about having a hair out of place or a wrinkle in a shirt—while never giving enough attention to finding their monologues.

Absolutely, a good headshot is critical. It is your calling card, your introduction to the people who can give you work. But once they've "met" you on paper, what will you show them in person?

When you walk into an audition, you need to feel prepared and confident about *all* of your audition tools: your great headshot, your effective résumé, *and* your prepared monologue. The quality of your monologue shows the casting people more than your acting talent; it tells them whether or not they can put their confidence in you as a reliable, focused, "thinking" actor.

To help you deliver a winning performance, this section:

1. Describes the process of finding a monologue that suits you

2. Explains how to prepare the text of your monologue for an audition

3. Gets your monologue up on its feet with advice about staging

4. Helps you focus on your objective and your imaginary scene partner

5. Explores the ways in which you can make your piece shine and show off who you are

WHAT IS A MONOLOGUE?

"Monologue" means "to speak alone"; it comes from the Greek word *monologos*. A monologue can be a section of a play, a movie, or a book; a speech; or a continuous series of jokes, ideas, thoughts, or stories told by one person. For your audition monologue you may use a single paragraph or section of lines in a script, or you may put together several short lines that progress as if they had been written as one unit.

A monologue audition is a very special and specific kind of performance. You have only a fleeting amount of time to introduce yourself and to exhibit your talent. You have no support onstage—no actors, no props, no context—and your auditors have your fate in their hands. Watching you is their job, and they're working under stress. The pressure is enormous for all of you, and this unique situation requires a unique performance approach. In an audition, you can't simply expect to show up with even a great speech from a role that brought you the acclaim of a paying audience and expect it to work *as is*. Some of those great speeches never work as audition pieces. After reading this section of the *Commonsense Guide*, you'll know how to find the ones that do.

CHAPTER 13

Finding a Monologue

THE BASICS

Keep in mind that using a monologue for the purpose of an audition is artificial. Playwrights and screenwriters don't write monologues into their scripts thinking, "This monologue will make a good audition piece." Their monologues are written in the service of the whole script. When you excerpt a monologue from a script for an audition, you need to remember that you don't have the advantage of the full story that the script offers. You can't rely on your audience (the casting director, director, and/or producer) knowing the character's story or obstacles, intentions, and actions. In a lot of ways, the monologue for an audition needs to be approached as if it were its own play, with its own sense of beginning, middle, and end.

TIME

Now let's talk about the length of your little "play." A monologue used for an audition should be *no longer than two minutes.* This is the usual limit for professional auditions, although you should be prepared for situations in which you're allowed as little as one minute, or are asked to perform two monologues within a longer amount of time. In any case, two minutes should be the maximum you allow for a monologue. Be strict about this! If you go beyond two minutes, the auditors might start to squirm in their chairs, or cut you off. And the closer you get to that magic two-minute mark, the less likely it is that you'll have their attention—because they'll be worrying about your going over. Casting directors can see hundreds of people in a single day. They have tight schedules, and have been trained to assess your work in only a very brief audition.

When choosing monologues, a good range of time to aim for is no less than one minute and no more than two, when performed. "When performed" means when you are acting it, fully memorized, with staging. You can identify a two-minute monologue by the length of the text. Generally, a two-minute monologue has anywhere from twenty to thirty-five sentences, although there are always exceptions. (Twenty sentences in *Major Barbara*, for instance, would probably be a lot longer than twenty sentences in *Waiting for Godot.*)

A monologue on the page will always be longer when performed. So reading your monologue out loud in a chair in your living room will only give you an *idea* of how long it is, because you haven't added any stage business yet. The only true way to know the timing of your monologue is to time yourself while performing it. This can be done in your apartment as well as on a stage—just make sure you are performing the role with as much energy as you will use when you are in that audition room in front of the auditors.

MULTIPLE CHOICES

It is always a good thing for an actor to have a variety of monologues rehearsed and ready to go. That way you are prepared for any type of audition. At a minimum, you should have six to ten fully memorized pieces. I recommend two to four dramatic pieces, two to four comedic pieces, and two to four classical pieces (two comedic, two dramatic). Most acting schools and regional theater auditions will ask for two contrasting monologues: those could be a comedic and a dramatic, a contemporary and a classical, or some other contrasting combination. Most young actors go to Shakespeare's plays for their classical selections, but "classical" includes many more writers than the Bard. Generally, this category is defined as beginning with the Greeks and Romans, and concluding about the end of the nineteenth century. In between you can choose from Shakespeare and his contemporaries, Restoration playwrights, French writers ranging from Racine to Molière, and the Edwardians. Among those who might be considered *semi*-classical authors are Ibsen, Strindberg, and Oscar Wilde.

GET EXCITED!

Now, begin the monologue process by thinking about playwrights and screenplays (or books, poets, or musicians) that excite you. What is it about each that stimulates you? Which books, poets, or musicians do you identify with? Who speaks the way you speak, thinks the way you think? Are there characters who you can see yourself playing? Do you watch, read, or listen to a work and exclaim, "This is a great role! I could really see myself playing it"?

FOLLOW THE PATH TO THE WRITER

Once you've found a work that you've connected with, devour every play, song, book, or film by its writer. Chances are good that you can use a monologue from one of this person's texts. You might even be able to find a great monologue from a lesser-known play. This would give you an important advantage over actors who are auditioning with the same old monologues that have been used for years.

What if you have gone forth, searched, and read twelve plays, three movie scripts, and two short books written by this exciting author and have found . . . that this person doesn't write monologues for his or her characters? Well, you have learned something important! You've learned that you are attracted to the *style* of the playwright. Once you have identified the style you like, you can try to find other authors who write in it as well. As you read this playwright who excites you, what sorts of adjectives come to mind?

Here are three examples of playwrights and some language that could describe their styles:

1. David Mamet: fast paced and clipped

2. Suzan-Lori Parks: full of metaphor and playful

3. Tennessee Williams: graceful and expressive

Maybe it's not the dialogue that attracts you. Other reasons you might be drawn to a playwright's style include the characters that have been created or the environment in which the plays take place. Identifying these characteristics can help in your search for an audition piece that excites you.

TYPE AND YOUR MONOLOGUE

You'll hear the word "type" often. It's a shortcut word that people in the business use when trying to match an actor to a role: "What we need is a Cate Blanchett type," or, "No, I think he's more of a Billy Bob Thornton type"; or, perhaps, "I want a hard-driving lawyer type," or, "I'm looking for a compassionate nurse type."

Instead of asking what "type" you are, let's turn the question around: what type of role can you play? Probably *many* types, but there are also many types that you clearly and realistically will not be asked to play. As you build your career, it's important for you to figure out which is which. You don't want to waste your time and the auditors' by responding to a casting call that you are totally wrong for. If, for example, the casting notice calls for a Jennifer Aniston type, and you are a Robert De Niro type, you'd be crazy to show up at the audition. If you're a short, overweight, balding man in his fifties, you're not going to answer a casting call for a tall, twenty-something, clean-shaven blond-haired guy.

On the other hand, if the script—or the casting notice—doesn't limit you, don't limit yourself. For instance, who says that a "hard-driving lawyer" can't be a fragile-looking young woman? Or that a "compassionate nurse" can't be a stocky, middle-aged man? If the casting notice is more specific, and asks for a hard-driving, middle-aged male lawyer, or for a compassionate, frail, young female nurse—then the options, and your suitability, are much more limited.

The casting process is complex; at times it can look arbitrary or indecisive. You'll never be able to get inside an auditor's head and know exactly what he or she wants. Often the auditor doesn't know for sure, even after publishing a very specific casting notice. The producers of *Death of a Salesman* wanted a runt of a man to create the role of Willy Loman, but cast big, hulking Lee J. Cobb after seeing him audition.

It's frustrating when casting directors are unshakable in their insistence that, for example, young lovers should always be slender and good looking, or the heavy should be big and burly. These are conventions that audiences expect and accept.

Whatever the casting people do with the information you give them, it's important for you to know what they see when you walk in the door, and what you present to them in your audition. Casting for commercials and episodic television relies greatly on the auditors' first impression of you. These are visual mediums, so—especially in commercials—actors have no time to make anything *but* a first impression on the viewers. Theater and film can afford to be subtler. People who are casting for these auditions will be studying the many "colors" that you play and noting the range of emotions and situations that you can handle. (See "Colors of the Monologue," page 80). Be aware of this when you're selecting your audition monologues, and think about what aspects of yourself you'll want to show the casting people. Know what type you're auditioning for and ask yourself whether you're a good fit. The characteristics of each part that you're going up for will determine which of your strengths and colors you'll want to stress in that particular audition. That's why you want at *least* half a dozen different monologues; you'll never find just one contemporary and one classic monologue that work optimally for every audition.

It's easier to know what the part you're going for demands if you can read the script in advance and note what other people in the play have to say about "your" character. When all you have to go on is a brief casting notice, your job is harder, but not impossible. You need to study the notice to learn everything you can about the project and the role. Using that information, you figure out as best you can which of your monologues is most likely to show the auditors that you can play this type of character.

MONOLOGUE BOOKS

Monologue books, which compile monologues from plays and movies, are an obvious starting point for finding pieces spoken by types you may be asked to play. Many of these books are available in stores and on the Internet. If you are fortunate enough to live in an area that has a performing arts bookstore, you should use it as a resource. The bigger chain bookstores, like Barnes & Noble and Borders, carry some of these books in their performing arts sections. On the Internet, sites like Amazon.com can be very useful. And your local library should be considered, as many libraries can now locate and borrow books for you from other libraries all over the world.

These monologue books are usually paperbacks and are compiled in categories. Their titles might resemble these: *The Best Monologues from 2005*, *Monologues for Men Age Twenty to Thirty*, *Comedic Young Women Monologues from Shakespeare*, and *The Best Dramatic Children's Monologues from 2003*. Start looking through these books to get a feel for which monologues you like and which you don't, and to find those that suit you.

Most of the monologues in these books fit the two-minute time frame that casting directors usually ask for. (Later in this section we'll discuss how to cut down a piece that is too long.) Isolate those monologues that remind you of you or jump out and grab you. Trust your instincts and don't censor yourself. If you come across a monologue that speaks to you, for whatever reason, keep it as a possible choice for your list of monologues. Later you can shorten that list, but it is always, *always* better to have more choices than fewer. Make a second list, of types of characters, plays, and playwrights that you want to investigate further.

You can also benefit from exploring monologues that aren't an obvious match for your physical type. I encourage you to research pieces that interest you even if the character who delivers them is of your opposite sex, or of a different age or ethnicity. Sometimes such a monologue can work for you if its language and style are not gender, age, or race specific, and especially if the play from which it has been taken is not well known. Sometimes altering just one word (changing "he" to "she") can do the trick.

A cautionary note about monologue books: because these are readily available, too many actors (the lazier or less savvy ones) get their monologues from them. That means that by the time you walk into your audition, the auditors have already heard the monologue you are going to do—many times! Nothing grabs the interest of a casting director more than a new, well-acted selection. Separate yourself from the rest of the crowd by finding a monologue that isn't overdone. *Monologue books should be used only as a guide*—a jumping-off point. Challenge yourself to look for something that isn't in those books. However, if after you have searched elsewhere, you still feel that the best selection for you is in one of those books, then go for it. Your best audition will be with a monologue you like and are comfortable and confident with. Chapter 19 lists some overused monologues that you really should avoid.

The monologue research process works for you on many positive levels. Not only are you finding your piece, but you are exposing yourself to more plays and playwrights. Think of this as an archeological dig: you are going to discover some interesting pieces; most will be broken and unusable, but dig long enough and you will locate a real treasure. Most people don't really take the time necessary to find the right piece. Remember those students of mine who spent weeks and months getting their headshots ready, but put barely any time into finding and preparing monologues? Monologue hunting can be a very lengthy process. Give yourself plenty of time. It *always* takes longer than you think!

MAKE THE JOURNEY

Most importantly, when deciding on a monologue, you should ask yourself, what kind of journey does this monologue take? Is it a worthy journey that will engage and take the auditors with you through all of its peaks and valleys' twists and turns? Or is the trip over in the first few sentences, leaving you and the casting people on a barren plateau for the next minute and a half? A good audition monologue should always have a strong journey with a beginning, middle, and end. Is your entire expedition only a walk to the front porch for the morning newspaper, or will you have to struggle ten miles in a snowstorm to get that paper? Which journey seems more interesting? Which story has more acting choices? Which has a more defined beginning, middle, and end? My money is on the second.

Think about your monologue as if it were a piece of music. How long would you want to listen to a song if the chords didn't change, or if the singer kept singing the same lines over and over again? To catch your auditors' ears, find a piece that uses all of the notes on the scale, and that combines them in unexpected and intriguing progressions.

WHAT'S ON THE LINE? WHAT'S AT STAKE?

Having a strong journey in your monologue depends in part on having strong stakes. Choose a monologue that gives you a compelling reason to talk. Ask yourself: "What is on the line with this monologue?" "What do I want from my imaginary scene partner—how do I need to change him or her?" "Is my need to speak important enough to keep the casting director interested in my story and in watching me?"

Going out on the porch to get yourself the paper on a lazy, sunny morning while you wonder aloud what you'll do today doesn't put much on the line. But if your husband will beat you to a pulp if you don't get the morning paper, if the closest newsstand is ten miles down the mountain, a major snowstorm is gathering, and you have to persuade your imaginary scene partner to drive you to town. . . . Now, that's a monologue with a journey and with life-or-death high stakes! That's a monologue worth telling.

COLORS OF THE MONOLOGUE

Theater people talk about the emotional colors in a scene or monologue. "Color" is the variety of the character's emotional response to a situation. A good monologue will give you a rich variety of sensations to work with, which will lead you to a multicolored performance. Think of your monologue as a painting. How many different colors in it can you identify? Is your monologue only one shade of brown, or of blue, or of red? What effect will that single color have on your performance? One color equals one acting choice. If your two-minute monologue has only one color, you will be playing one acting choice for two minutes. That is the entire range of emotions that the auditors will see. Is that all you want to show of your acting talents?

How do you find a monologue with more than one color? Again, look for pieces with strong journeys and high stakes—almost always they'll give you the chance to explore a rainbow of colors honestly. Complex and conflicted characters offer an even wider range of colors to play with.

Your overall objective as a monologue hunter is to find a compelling journey, high stakes, and a vivid color spectrum. Your monologue doesn't have to be about a life-or-death situation, but it does need these three criteria to capture the auditors: (1) strong journey, (2) strong stakes, and (3) strong range of colors.

MAKE IT YOUR BUSINESS TO KNOW PLAYS!

Most young actors don't read enough. But as an actor you need to be in the know, and part of your job is to know *plays*. Read as many of them as you can—make it a ritual. Many publications cover the plays that are currently being produced and published. *The Sunday New York Times* "Arts and Leisure" section should be read every week. Theatre Communications Group's monthly *American Theatre* magazine tracks productions at regional companies throughout the country. Reading trade papers for the performing arts, like *Back Stage* or *PerformInk*, should be part of your routine. Add script-reading times to your weekly schedule and adhere to them; read *at least* three plays a week. Make this a part of your actor training.

If you want the edge that your competition already has, you need to keep yourself up-to-date and knowledgeable about the world of theater: about the plays being done, their writers, directors, and production companies. The more you know, the more confident and prepared you will be as an actor. Familiarizing yourself with a wide range of plays also exposes you to potential audition material.

Whenever possible, make sure that you have read the play from which your audition monologue comes. True, new scripts are not always available for auditionees to study, but at the very least you should *always* know the title of the play and the names of your character and the playwright. You would be surprised at how many actors forget to memorize this information!

FINDING A MONOLOGUE THAT IS UNIQUE

Maybe you have found a playwright whose work you like but who has no monologues that fit your type—or is so popular that his or her plays are overused for auditions. For example, suppose you really admire David Mamet's writing. You love his plays, you love his movies, but you can't seem to find an appropriate monologue in them for your auditions. Look for a lesser-known playwright whose style and feel resemble Mamet's. You will probably find more than a few, because Mamet has been writing for over twenty years. That's enough time for younger playwrights to be influenced by the music he has created. After all, there are only so many notes to go around; sooner or later you can hear almost the same song, just played a little differently, by other writers.

I CAN'T FIND ANY MONOLOGUES I LIKE

Finding a monologue in which every word and moment fits you perfectly is almost impossible. But this doesn't mean you won't find a great monologue that completely works for you. Lower your standards just a bit by locating a monologue that is *almost perfect* for you. Keep reading, keep looking, and keep yourself open to all the possibilities. If finding a monologue that you like takes a long time, that's good. It means that you are being very specific and particular about what you are looking for. If, on the other hand, you feel like you are "settling" with a certain monologue, you probably are.

OTHER SOURCES

Books, poems, songs, magazines, editorials—and, of course, films: monologues pop up in the strangest places. If you are looking for something new, you must be open to all possibilities, and sometimes scenes from these sources can be adapted for theater auditions. For example, every now and then a book comes along that is written in such a way that it transfers from the page to the stage rather easily.

A few years ago, a student whom I was working with brought in a monologue that fit him like a glove. It was wonderful: exciting and dramatic, with comic moments. And fresh—I had never heard it before. When I asked where he got it, he hesitated to reveal that it came from a book: *Midnight in the Garden of Good and Evil*. A year later, I went out to see a movie made from a book called—you guessed it—*Midnight in the Garden of Good and Evil*. There was Kevin Spacey performing the same monologue taken directly from the book. My student had been ahead of the game; until the movie came out, he had a unique monologue. Unfortunately, after the film's release he had to find a new piece because this one was no longer unusual, and because auditors now connected it with Kevin Spacey. This kind of turnover is part of the game of auditioning.

Poems also can be adapted into audition monologues. Contemporary poets shouldn't be overlooked; consider the popularity of "poetry slams." Russell Simmons' *Def Poetry Jam*, which ran on Broadway and subsequently aired on HBO, featured several performers reciting their own poems, which often felt like monologues.

An alternative to a classical monologue could be a Shakespearean sonnet. The Bard wrote more than one hundred of these fourteen-line poems, and some are not well known. You can also take a look at Ben Johnson's or Christopher Marlowe's poetry, among others'. Expand your scope. Any of these poems could show off your ability to handle a heightened text.

One example of a songwriter who often sings in the style of a theatrical monologue is Tom Waites; his lyrics might be used as material for your auditions. Musical theater is a great, rarely tapped source for monologues. Most people only look at nonmusicals, so they miss out on a wide range of possibilities. Read the texts of musicals—from *Assassins* to *The Fantasticks*, and from *Runaways* to *Working*—maybe a slight cut-and-paste will create your next audition piece.

Comedians are another good source of material. Dozens of published books and discs feature standup rants from comedians of all ethnicities and cultures. Could part of a comic routine be turned into a monologue? If you aren't a funny person, look for a comedian's serious or vulnerable moments. Sometimes these are masked by humor; sometimes they're nakedly dramatic. (It is my belief that the best dramatic actors *must* have a solid sense of humor.) You can also take most comedic pieces and make them dramatic. Think about it.

Editorials can be unexpected treasures. Take a satiric piece that appeared during George W. Bush's first term as president, about his secretary of defense, Donald Rumsfeld. The editorial was written as if Rumsfeld were ordering a "Grand Slam Breakfast" at a Denny's restaurant. It satirized his particular way of speaking and the amount of time it might take him to order something as simple as breakfast. It was a perfect monologue: funny, intelligent, and serious, with a great flow and rhythm to the language, and a solid journey. It was written to be read, but was screaming to be performed! With a few small cuts for time, this editorial would have been an excellent audition piece. (Note, though, that editorials by nature tend to be topical, so an audition based on one may not be usable for long.)

CAUTION

Remember that screenplays, books, songs, poems, standup comedy routines, and editorials were not written as audition monologues for the theater. They were crafted for other genres, and although they may succeed brilliantly in their original forms, they might not translate well into your two minutes of performance. Judge them by the same criteria that you would judge a passage from a play: does this piece work out of context? Are my stakes high enough? What do I need from my imaginary scene partner? Are there many colors? You won't be applauded for finding a unique audition monologue if it doesn't work in an audition.

A monologue taken from a movie or song can be tricky in another way: it may be too thoroughly associated with an established actor, singer, or character. For instance, a few years ago one of my students brought in a monologue from the movie *A Time to Kill*. He did a wonderful acting job. His performance was vulnerable, effective, and well paced. The only problem was that this student (I'll call him Lex) looked nothing like Matthew McConaughey, who played the role in the movie. I felt strongly that casting people might be confused by Lex's monologue choice. Because his monologue did not fit him physically, using it would send them mixed signals. They might practically and logically ask, "Do you want to be considered for Matthew McConaughey roles?" His answer would be no; he wanted to be considered for roles on the basis of his own work, choices, and type. Lex understood my point, but decided to use the monologue for an upcoming audition.

Lex performed his *A Time to Kill* monologue in a New York City presentation for casting directors, agents, and directors. He was one of several actors presenting their audition pieces in this performance "showcase." The auditors gave their feedback in writing, and some of them had stinging opinions of Lex's selection. One wrote only five words—"You are no Matthew McConaughey"—but gave no response to the monologue itself or to its performance. Another stated, "I could not get past thinking anything other than the fact that this is a Matthew McConaughey monologue." Lex was crushed. By choosing to audition with *A Time to Kill*, he had unintentionally told the auditors that he saw himself as a Matthew McConaughey type. All of his preparation and hard work had been wasted—not to mention the money he had paid for the package of classes that concluded with this showcase. He vowed that he would never again audition with that monologue.

You have two minutes in an audition to tell the casting people as much as you can about who you are, who you think you are, and what you are capable of. Agents, directors, and casting directors need your help to show them who you are so they can send you out for the roles that are right for you. Their own reputations depend on how accurately they gauge what you can do. Don't sabotage your audition by choosing inappropriate material.

Lex and I learned a lot from his showcase feedback. We started over and found monologues that had the same feel, style, and energy as the one he'd selected from *A Time to Kill*, but that weren't associated with a recognizable actor. Now when he auditions, he is clearly telling his auditors who he is and what kinds of roles he is right for.

DOES THIS MONOLOGUE WORK? A TRIAL RUN

"I swear it sounded much better when I was doing it at home." This is a common experience. Your monologue almost always sounds—and feels—better when you're acting it at home, alone. Home is a comfortable, familiar place where you feel safe. The true test of whether a piece works in an audition is to get it up on its feet in a performance space, in front of an audience.

Once you've memorized and rehearsed what you think is a perfect monologue, you need to act it in front of someone—ideally outside of your home, in a performance space. Bring the piece into a classroom, a studio, or a theater. Get at least one person to watch you and give you feedback. Placing yourself in a space outside of your own comfort zone, and giving yourself an audience, tests both you and your monologue. Your performance will feel different in this situation, which resembles the audition itself. It's best to discover that difference, and your reaction to it, under relatively friendly circumstances. You don't want the casting director to be your first audience for a monologue. And you don't want to find out at the audition that your monologue doesn't work.

GUIDELINES

No steadfast rule determines which monologues work and which don't. Whether or not a given monologue succeeds can depend totally on the unique character traits of the individual who is performing it. But the following guidelines can help you avoid monologues with trouble spots that make them hard to pull off.

Keep It Present

Look for monologues that take place in the present or that have a present-tense feel. Read these two examples of one monologue. Each uses a different tense. Which one is more engaging for the actor to perform and for the audience to watch?

- I was eight years old when my father took me to the zoo. I saw elephants and zebras. I remember it was a hot day and I remember sweating. I ran away from my father.

- I am eight years old; my father and I are at the zoo. I see elephants and zebras. I am hot, sweating; I run away from my father.

Which one feels more exciting, more open to any possibility? The second one, right? What's the difference? The first choice is what I refer to as lean-back acting—meaning the energy isn't forward and engaging. Steer clear of these "I remember when" monologues. Using the past tense forces you to make acting choices that are all stuck . . . well, in the past. Throughout your performance you'll be trying "to remember," trying "to recall." That makes for a *boring* audition!

Now, what about the second version? There's no need to remember or to recall here. Even though you're a grown-up telling a story about a past event, you are *presently reliving every moment*, and you aren't relying on weak past-tense verbs. Because you are in the present tense, you have to make active choices about how you move through space and how you interact with other characters. Moment by moment, you and your audience are presently engaged in events that are actively and organically occurring right before your eyes and theirs.

Here is an example of an exciting monologue that occurs in real time; it's in the present and automatically brings the audience/auditor along for every moment of the ride:

Jack and Jill
By Jane Martin
JACK: Listen, I've been . . . one minute of your time . . . sitting over there, and I . . . no place is safe, right? I'm sorry. By the way, you're reading a poet I admire. . . In the face of that tragic life, she . . . wait, wait, I'm backing up here . . . I was, from over there in the stacks, struck, struck by you . . . viscerally struck . . . as if you cared, right? Why, why am I . . . look, I'm Jack, unpronounceable second last name . . . we

could . . . well, this is fairly mortifying. Let me try to do this without artifice . . . I'm going to erase this desperate preamble and, uh, say this: I, Jack, would like to meet you, a female person, for . . . ummm, non-threatening relating. Why? Because a while ago I lost some serious relating, and I really miss the feeling. So, severe and transcendent beauty, how about a cup of coffee with me, Jack Stojadinovac? (Pause) I have this . . . intuition . . . that I am dog meat.

Think about this monologue as if you were an actor rehearsing it for auditions. How does your imaginary scene partner react to what you are saying? How many different "actable" choices can you discover? The forward, present energy is built right into the text of this selection. As long as you are present and committed to your acting choices, the auditors can't lose interest, because you are making those choices this very moment, right in front of them.

Stay out of the Past

Now, let's take a look at two other brief monologues that talk about the past. [The "*" indicates where the paragraph has been cut.]

Greensboro
By Emily Mann

JANE: *When I was about eight, I remember my mother told me she wanted to show me something. I can see the picture in my mind of her taking me to this hall closet in our house and pulling out this Klan robe. My father was in the Klan. I remember being shocked. I don't remember having the sensibility to be offended . . . I was just shocked. There was a point where I realized what he was doing was very racist, but he was very loving.**

My mother was one of these typical Southern religious women, very quiet. I remember thinking that if she ever had an independent thought in her life, I never knew what it was. She never talked about bigoted stuff; she just sort of nodded a lot.

Free Gift
By Israel Horovitz

HEATHER: *I remember going to a funeral of an old friend's father . . . in Brooklyn, when I was maybe twenty. Stephanie. Stephanie was somebody I went to first grade with . . . The father had been married before, a long time before he'd married the mother. We knew there was another daughter somewhere, but, we didn't know that the father had been keeping up with her, with this other daughter . . . keeping in touch . . . being a kind of daddy, on some level. At the funeral, the*

*casket was, you know, open. The father was dolled up in a blue suit
and red tie and his skin was kind of this weird gray/green color. He
was a really dark-skinned man, but you wouldn't've known this from
lookin' at him.*

What type of energy do these monologues have? Do they pop out at you and engage you, or do they reminisce with a lean-back energy (energy that isn't forward and engaging)? Low energy is built into both of these monologues. Look at their language. Note the words that creep into them: "I remember." "I was." "I realized." These verbs are similar; the actions that they will propel are similar; the range of colors that they will evoke is limited. These monologues may be well crafted and effective in the context of the plays that they were written for. But they carry many acting limitations as audition pieces.

Past-tense monologues force you to work much harder to keep them engaging and present. Again, I recommend that you avoid using past-tense selections— but if you must audition with one, figure out how to keep it as present as possible. Will changing a word or two make a difference? How can your physical blocking help?

Some monologues in the present include the telling of a story from the past. These shouldn't be dismissed as bad choices. They can be considered, but you need to identify the moment(s) when the speaker vividly remembers and/or enters into the past. Keep the energy moving forward and don't lean back into just comfortably recalling those good old days.

Here are three examples of monologues that dip into the past but stay in the present; they work as audition pieces because of their present-tense, forward energy.

The Rainmaker
By N. Richard Nash
*STARBUCK: I seen even better blessings, Lizzie-girl! I got a brother
who's a doctor. You don't have to tell him where you ache or where
you pain! He just comes in and lays his hand on your heart and pretty
soon you're breathin' sweet again. And I got another brother who can
sing—and when he's singin', that song is there!—and never leaves you!
I used to think—why ain't I blessed like Fred or Arny? Why am I just
a nothin' man, with nothin' special to my name? And then one summer
comes the drought—and Fred can't heal it away and Arny can't sing it
away! But me—I go down to the hollow and I look up and I say: "Rain!
Dammit!—please!—bring rain!" And the rain came! And I knew—
I knew I was one of the family! That's a story. You don't have to believe
it if you don't want to.*

Fences
By August Wilson

ROSE: I been standing with you! I been right here with you, Troy. I got a life, too. I gave eighteen years of my life to stand in the same spot with you. Don't you think I ever wanted other things? Don't you think I had dreams and hopes? What about my life? What about me? Don't you think it ever crossed my mind to want to know other men? That I wanted to lay up somewhere and forget about my responsibilities? That I wanted someone to make me laugh so I could feel good? You not the only one who's got wants and needs. But I held onto you, Troy. I took all my feelings, my wants and needs, my dreams . . . and I buried them inside you. I planted a seed and watched and prayed over it. I planted myself inside you, and waited to bloom. And it didn't take me no eighteen years to find out the soil was hard and rocky and it wasn't never gonna bloom.

But I held onto you, Troy. I held you tighter. You was my husband. I owed you everything I had. Every part of me I could find to give you. And upstairs in that room . . . with the darkness falling in on me . . . I gave everything I had to try and erase the doubt that you wasn't the finest man in the world. And wherever you was going . . . I wanted to be there with you. Cause you was my husband. Cause that's the only way I was gonna survive as your wife. You always talking about what you give . . . and what you don't have to give. But you take, too. You take . . . and don't even know nobody's giving!

Sunshine
By William Mastrosimone

NELSON: Her bicycle chain caught her jeans. Tumbles into the swimming pool. Bike dragged her right to the bottom. Never had a chance to cry out for Mommy. They always say the same thing: "I just went in the house for a second. We were gonna drain that pool next weekend." So you get there. You find signs of life. Evacuate the lungs. I.V. 'em. Throw the drug box at 'em. Every E.M.T. trick in the book and some you invented. You know how to save a life. You see a light flicker in the eyes and you work her hard and you keep working her hard even though you know she's been ten minutes without O_2 and the brain damage is massive, massive, but you keep working her and working her because you are there to save a life and goddammit them young lungs snap back into action and you get a pulse and her eyes light up and she pukes and coughs and cries like the day she was born and people cheer and hug you and thank you ten million times. You're a hero. You saved a cabbage that looks something like a six-year-old girl who ain't never going to *ride that bicycle again. Ain't ever going to run and play with her little playmates again. And her family's going broke for the rest of their lives to keep her lungs inflated. And when it's sunny, they'll strap her in a highchair on the front porch so she can watch other kids playing and she's there swinging her arms and drooling down her chin making sounds nobody understands. Or wants to. You've seen all this before. And no matter how many years you got on the job, none of it makes sense until it hits you one day you might do more good if, under pressure, you miscalculated the morphine dosage, put her in the back of the ambulance, let her mother hug her one last time, and make sure you catch every fucking red light from there to the emergency room so she's D.O.A.*

I was finished today when I had to pry her fingers off her doll.

Leave Dreams for Sleeping

A troubling piece to avoid is the dream monologue. It can start off in many ways, but it always has the same effect. "I had the craziest dream last night . . .," begins the character, who goes on for two pages (which would be at least four minutes in performance) about things that could only happen in a dream. The problem with these monologues is that the acting is unrealistic. The actor who chooses one of these is spreading him- or herself out with a crazy story, while at the same time limiting his or her acting colors. The only thing the auditor will hear is, ". . . and then this happened, and then I did this . . ." This type of monologue isn't a good choice for an audition.

Most dream monologues usually work within the context of the play because they have the benefit of story, and of characters to help prop it up. The audience is already deeply invested in the characters' journeys. Taken out of context, the dream or memory monologue is a confusing, useless journey that can never really show off an actor's talents to his or her best advantage. And what verb acting choices does it give you? "To recall." "To remember." Do you see a familiar limited pattern here?

Acknowledge a Bad Choice

If you do decide to try out one of these pieces set in the past or recounting a dream, *be very careful*. Make sure that the writing resists clichés. Make sure that you show your full emotional, vocal, and physical choices—a full range of colors. If you have tried everything you can and the piece still doesn't soar—acknowledge it! The best thing you can do for yourself is to move on. Sometimes your wonderful acting abilities can't (or can't honestly) overcome the blasé text of a monologue.

Avoid Rambling Monologues

These usually involve a character who is rambling on about many things that consume him. As the actor continues to rant in character, the viewer gets bored and confused by these words that seem to go nowhere. Such a monologue has no emotional journey and no stakes.

Don't Write Your Own Monologue

Now that you understand the structure of a good audition monologue, you may be thinking, "Hey, why don't I write my own monologue for auditions?" Good thought! *Bad* idea. Don't do it. Casting people want to see and hear you audition with a piece that is already published—or at least has a history of being produced. You immediately send the wrong message to the auditors by auditioning with a self-written monologue. They'll assume that you've tailored the piece to your own strengths, and will suspect the quality and range of your acting. But they sure won't question the size of your ego. You'll be telling them, "No text but my own writing was good enough for me." Big mistake!

Test Yourself: Is This Audition Material?

Take a look at this monologue from a Pulitzer Prize–winning play. Do you think it would make a good audition?

> *You and me. Nobody's going to look after us. Bradley can't look after us. Bradley can hardly look after himself. I was always hoping that Tilden would look out for Bradley when they got older. After Bradley lost his leg. Tilden's the oldest. I always thought he'd be the one to take responsibility. I had no idea in the world that Tilden would be so much trouble. Who would've dreamed. Tilden was an All-American, don't forget. Don't forget that. Fullback. Or quarterback. I forget which.*
>
> *Then when Tilden turned out to be so much trouble, I put all my hopes on Ansel. Of course Ansel wasn't as handsome, but he was smart. He was the smartest probably. I think he probably was. Smarter than Bradley, that's for sure. Didn't go and chop his leg off with a chain saw. Smart enough not to go and do that. I think he was smarter than Tilden, too. Especially after Tilden got in all that trouble. Doesn't take brains to go to jail. Anybody knows that. Course then when Ansel died that left us alone. Same as being alone. No different. Same as if they'd all died. He was the smartest. He could've earned lots of money. Lots and lots of money.*

Take a moment to think about what you remember from the monologue. Write down what your *instincts* tell you about the feel and energy of this piece. Which words stood out? Where do you imagine that this person is? Is he (or she) standing, or sitting? Who is the speaker talking to, and with what objective? Can this piece stand on its own? Does it have a strong enough journey with a beginning, middle, and end? Is there a payoff at the end that leaves the auditors with a strong sense of who you are, or does the writing fizzle out?

Is this a good audition piece? No!

Buried Child, the play from which this monologue is taken, and Sam Shepard, its author, come with many awards attached; Shepard is considered one of the best contemporary American writers in the last fifty years. But this piece is a *terrible* choice for an audition monologue.

If I were watching an actress (the character is a woman) auditioning with this piece, here is what I would focus on: a lot of names of people whom I don't know. I would be concentrating on catching up with what she is saying, rather than being absolutely present and watching her act! Bradley . . . Tilden . . . Ansel . . . somebody played football, somebody lost his leg, somebody was smart. Tilden went to jail, Ansel died, and this little piggy went to the market. You can't make this monologue "pop out and excite" when isolated as an audition piece. Move on! It belongs in the full-length play it was written for.

Consider Imagery and Poetry

You may come across a contemporary text that is poetic in its style and feel. Don't rule it out. This kind of monologue may be a perfect fit for you. Choosing one is similar to choosing any contemporary text: ask yourself, "Can I play/act this and make it work specifically and effectively?"

Here are monologues from two different Maria Irene Fornes plays. Both are written in a heightened poetic style. Decide whether either would be a good choice for an audition piece.

Promenade
By Maria Irene Fornes
MOTHER:
I saw a man lying in the street,
Asleep and drunk.
He had not washed his face.
He held his coat closed with a safety pin
And I thought, and I thought
Thank God, I'm better than he.

I have to live with my own truth,
I have to live with it.
You live with your own truth,
I cannot live with it.
I have to live with my own truth,
Whether you like it or not,
Whether you like it or not.

There are many poor people in the world,
Whether you like it or not.

There are many poor people in the world.
But I'm not one of them.
I'm not one of them.
Someone's been stealing my apples
But I'm not one of them,
I'm not one of them.

I know everything.
Half of it I really know,
The rest I make up,
The rest I make up.
Some things I'm sure of,
Of other things I'm too sure,
And of others I'm not sure at all.
People believe everything they hear,
Not what they see, not what they see.
People believe everything they hear;
But me, I see everything
Yes, I see everything.

The saddest day of my life was the day
That I pitied a despicable man.
And I've been sad ever since,
Yes, I've been sad ever since.
I'd like to go where a human being
Is not a strange thing,
Is not a strange thing.

When I go, no one will water my plants.
When I go, no one will water my plants.
No one . . . no one . . . no one . . .
Yes my children, you'll find evil . . . some other time. Good night.

The Danube
By Maria Irene Fornes
EVE: //This may be the last time I come here.// Here is where I first kissed
you.// I kissed you that day, you know.// I kissed you because I could not
help myself.// Now again I try to exert control over myself// and I can't.//
I know I look distressed.// I feel how my face quivers. And my blood feels
thin.// And I can hardly breathe. And my skin feels dry.// I have no power
to show something other than what I feel.// I am destroyed. And even if I
try,// my lips will not smile.// Instead I cling to you and make it harder for
you.// Leave now.// Leave me here looking at the leaves.// Good bye.// If I
don't look at you it may be that I can let you go.

Both selections are filled with poetic imagery, but only one should be used as an audition monologue. *Promenade* takes a journey with a small number of colors and choices. The speaker is in distress and needs to have some questions answered. *The Danube* has a stronger journey with more specific colors and choices. *The Danube* is cleaner and shorter. *Promenade* is too long to be performed in a two-minute time frame. With *Danube*, an actor can make strong, specific technical choices. *Promenade* feels redundant and is limited by the speaker's lack of sureness. The actable choices aren't strong enough to show the casting director what you are really capable of. *The Danube* character, although using imagery and poetics, is speaking very specifically. Her throughline is clear and very actable on many specific levels. Every sentence/line is filled with one or more moments of colorful acting choices.

So, knowing that Maria Irene Fornes writes in a poetic style, can you use one of her monologues for auditions? Yes, you can, as long as you know what you are auditioning for. Ask yourself, "Does the style and feel of my monologue fit this particular role or show?"

Keep It Active

Often actors choose monologues that have an okay journey in terms of text, some colors, and some low-level stakes. With such pieces, the best that an actor can deliver is a satisfactory performance. An okay monologue is not what you want. Don't settle for what I call "CAB": clear, actable, but boring. A CAB monologue is understandable and clear, and its performer has made some okay acting choices. But the auditor has been bored because he or she got nothing from it: there was no soul, no spirit, and nothing particularly moving or memorable about what you did. In short, the auditor was bored because the monologue was boring.

If the monologue doesn't offer enough for you to act, find another piece. It's not enough for you to be a character who talks about the time your mother committed suicide—it's not enough if that's *all* you're talking about. The casting director will be thinking: "All right, your mother committed suicide; we got that in the first two lines. What else do you want to tell us?" A monologue with a strong journey and colors should always be an active heart beating, not a flatline.

MATCH YOUR MONOLOGUE TO THE JOB

Don't forget to do your homework on the audition itself. What exactly do the casting people want to see?

Are you auditioning for a single role in one play? If the script is available, make sure that you have read it and that you know something about the character. Ideally you'll have (or will have time to find and rehearse) a character/monologue that is similar—in personality and in emotional coloring and progression—to the role you're pursuing. Usually, the casting person will not want to see a monologue from the same play for which you are auditioning.

I'm afraid we have another lifeless audition on our hands!

You should be well informed so that you can make sensible, productive decisions about your audition material. If you are going to audition for Aaron Sorkin's *A Few Good Men*, for example, you will have read the play and familiarized yourself with Sorkin's style. You will understand that he writes in a straightforward manner with very little subtext and poetry. Knowing this, you would not commit audition suicide by showing up with a monologue that is poetic or texturally heightened. *A Few Good Men* is not the place for Fornes.

Are the casting people auditioning for an entire season of summer stock in which each actor will play several roles? First get the titles of the shows. Then attempt to find at least a plot summary and character breakdown for each, and try to decide which parts suit you best. When you're auditioning for several roles, it's unlikely that a single monologue can reflect the qualities of all of them. In this situation, choose a piece from your repertoire that best displays your emotional and technical range. (Alternatively, you may be asked for two contrasting selections.)

Having at least six to ten fully memorized monologues ready to go at all times keeps your options open, and keeps you on your toes. Remember that your choice of monologue must be as well thought out as anything else you do to prepare for an audition. What you've chosen gives the auditors a very strong clue as to who you are. If you walk into the audition with an inappropriate selection, you're telling the casting people that you have not researched the script and character that you're auditioning for, haven't understood what you've read, or have been too lazy to build a full repertoire of monologues.

Again, make sure your repertoire is fresh and that you haven't taken shortcuts to create it. If your monologue is straight out of a well-worn monologue book from your local library, you can bet money that the auditors have seen your choice before. It will scream out to the casting people that you didn't have time to find a monologue; you just grabbed what was in front of you. Make your auditors look up from their notebooks to ask where you found your unique piece. Then you will really have told them something about yourself!

CHAPTER 14

Preparing the Text

TAILORING YOUR PIECE TO FIT THE TIME LIMIT

If you have discovered a wonderful monologue that is too long for audition purposes, you may still be able to use it. A simple cut-and-paste job could be your solution. Begin by pulling out the material that isn't needed for your character's journey. What sections of this monologue seem redundant, unnecessary, or unactable? Where is the drop in the flow and energy of the text?

Some people in the acting world feel that editing the text of a playwright is blasphemy. But I am not suggesting that you rewrite your monologue; I *am* recommending that you find ways to tailor it to fit the constraints of an audition. Think of trimming your monologue as being a lot like finding the right sixteen bars of music. If, however, you do find yourself rewriting so much that your monologue no longer feels like the playwright's words, you should look for a more suitable audition piece. I believe that most monologues can be tailored to your specifications without taking anything away from the integrity of the character, or the text.

Here are some examples of how to cut down a monologue:

Blithe Spirit
By Noël Coward
CHARLES: Ruth—Elvira—are you there? Ruth—Elvira—I know damn well you're there—I just want to tell you that I am going away so there's no point in your hanging about any longer—I'm going a long way away—somewhere where I don't believe you'll be able to follow me. Is that quite clear, my darlings? In spite of what Elvira said I don't think spirits can travel over water. Is that quite clear, my darlings? You said in one of your acid moments, Ruth, that I had been hag-ridden all my life! How right you were—but now I'm free, Ruth dear, not only of mother and Elvira and Mrs. Winthrop-Lewellen, but free of you, too, and I should like to take this farewell opportunity of saying I'm enjoying it immensely—[A vase crashes into the fireplace]—Aha—I thought so— you were very silly, Elvira, to imagine that I didn't know all about Captain Bracegirdle—I did. But what you didn't know was that I was extremely attached to Paula Westlake at the time! [The clock strikes sixteen very viciously and very quickly] I was reasonably faithful to you, Ruth, but I doubt if it would have lasted much longer—you were

becoming increasingly domineering, you know, and there's nothing more off-putting than that, is there? [A large picture falls down with a crash] *Good-bye for the moment, my dears. I expect we are bound to meet again one day, but until we do I'm going to enjoy myself as I've never enjoyed myself before. You can break up the house as much as you like—I'm leaving it anyhow. Think kindly of me and send out good thoughts—*[The overmantel begins to shake and tremble as though someone were tugging at it]*—Nice work, Elvira—persevere. Good-bye again—parting is such* sweet *sorrow!*

The time for this monologue when performed is over two and a half minutes—too long for the usually allotted audition time. There are several ways to tailor this *Blithe Spirit* excerpt to your needs. For me, the easiest and cleanest cut would look like this:

CHARLES: *Ruth—Elvira—are you there? Ruth—Elvira—I know damn well you're there—I just want to tell you that I am going away so there's no point in your hanging about any longer—I'm going a long way away—somewhere where I don't believe you'll be able to follow me. Is that quite clear, my darlings? You said in one of your acid moments, Ruth, that I had been hag-ridden all my life! How right you were— but now I'm free, Ruth dear, not only of mother and Elvira and Mrs. Winthrop-Lewellen, but free of you, too, and I should like to take this farewell opportunity of saying I'm enjoying it immensely. I was reasonably faithful to you, Ruth, but I doubt if it would have lasted much longer—you were becoming increasingly domineering, you know, and there's nothing more off-putting than that, is there? Good-bye for the moment, my dears. I expect we are bound to meet again one day, but until we do I'm going to enjoy myself as I've never enjoyed myself before. You can break up the house as much as you like—I'm leaving it anyhow. Think kindly of me and send out good thoughts. Good-bye again— parting is such* sweet *sorrow!*

The monologue still flows, and for an audition is cleaner and much clearer. Its performance time is now about one minute forty-five seconds—well under the two-minute time constraint.

Here are the sections that have been cut from the original script:

In spite of what Elvira said I don't think spirits can travel over water. Is that quite clear, my darlings?

—[*A vase crashes into the fireplace*]—Aha—I thought so—you were very silly, Elvira, to imagine that I didn't know all about Captain Bracegirdle—I did. But what you didn't know was that I was extremely attached to Paula Westlake at the time! [*The clock strikes sixteen very viciously and very quickly*]

[*A large picture falls down with a crash*]

—[*The overmantel begins to shake and tremble as though someone were tugging at it*]— Nice work, Elvira—persevere.

Within the context of the play, that last deleted section is a fun actor moment. In an audition monologue, however, without the benefit of special effects and story line, it would be confusing.

DIALOGUE FOR ONE

Often a good audition piece can be crafted from a dialogue in a play. The second character's lines are edited out so that your character's lines become one continuous monologue. As you would in any scene that was originally written as a monologue, you'll be "interrupted" only by the reactions of your scene partner. In any audition monologue, that scene partner, and her reactions, are imaginary. Here is a very obvious example of this kind of editing:

The Shadow Box
By Michael Cristofer
BRIAN: . . . *people don't want to let go. Do they?*

VOICE OF INTERVIEWER: *How do you mean, Brian?*

BRIAN: *They think it's a mistake, they think it's supposed to last forever. I'll never understand that. My God, it's the one thing in this world you can be sure of! No matter what you do, no matter anything—sooner or later—it's going to happen. You're going to die. . . . And that's a relief— if you think about it. I should say if you think clearly about it.*

VOICE OF INTERVIEWER: *I'm not sure I follow you.*

BRIAN: *Well, the trouble is that most of us spend our entire lives trying to forget that we're going to die. And some of us even succeed. It's like pulling the cart without the horse. Or is that a poor analogy?*

VOICE OF INTERVIEWER: *No, Brian, I think it's fine.*

BRIAN: *Well, you get the gist of it anyway. I am afraid I've really lost touch with my words. They don't add up as neatly as they used to.*

VOICE OF INTERVIEWER: But you're still writing.

Here is what the monologue for Brian might look like, if you were to cut the Voice of the Interviewer's lines:

> BRIAN: *People don't want to let go. Do they? They think it's a mistake, they think it's supposed to last forever. I'll never understand that. My God, it's the one thing in this world you can be sure of! No matter who you are, what you do, no matter anything—sooner or later—it's going to happen. You're going to die. . . . And that's a relief—if you think about it. I should say if you think clearly about it. The trouble is that most of us spend our entire lives trying to forget that we're going to die. And some of us even succeed. It's like pulling the cart without the horse. Or is that a poor analogy?*
>
> *Well, you get the gist of it anyway. I am afraid I've really lost touch with my words. They don't add up as neatly as they used to. But I'm still writing.*

The Interviewer's lines have been cut, except for one, which is now the button at the end. It has been given to Brian simply by changing one word. "But you're still writing" has become, "But I'm still writing."

These monologues, created from *Blithe Spirit* and *The Shadow Box*, were chosen specifically because they are strong examples of how to pull a monologue from a full script. However, neither is recommended as an audition monologue. Here's why.

Blithe Spirit forces the actor playing Charles to deal with two ghosts that are constantly on the move. As the actor tries to see his two imaginary scene partners, his auditors will be confused and distracted: they'll wonder what he is doing, and probably will assume that he doesn't know *how* to focus or to concentrate onstage.

Brian's newly created monologue from *The Shadow Box* does not have a strong enough actable journey and offers few acting colors. It might be made to work if the stakes were incredibly high—if, for instance, this was Brian's last chance to make himself clear to the Interviewer before dying—and if, instead of relaying an opinion that he's formed in the past, Brian is grasping for and discovering each idea in the present.

CHAPTER 15

Creating the Scene

ESTABLISH THE ENVIRONMENT

In an audition situation you must be as strong and specific as possible. This helps you to focus and to draw your auditors into your scene. The more thoroughly you can imagine your surroundings, the more "in" the scene you will be, and the less you'll be distracted by nerves and surprises. Know exactly where you are during your performance; don't hurt yourself or confuse the casting director by forgetting about the specific environment in which it takes place! If your monologue is set in a barren cornfield in November, you need to "see" that cornfield. If your mono-logue occurs at a busy city street crossing on a scalding hot day in July, *if you do your job right*, the auditor will see and feel that cityscape through you.

TO WHOM ARE YOU SPEAKING?

Darren and I have both frequently mentioned the imaginary scene partner in your audition. You should have one. You've probably heard the saying, "Acting is reacting." Well, there's a lot of truth in that. It's not enough to have high stakes, a specific objec-tive, and wide-ranging colors if you're talking to empty space. You need to be specific here, too: you need to know to whom you're talking, and what response you're trying to get from your scene partner. That is, how do you want to change this person by your words and actions? Watch your partner like a hawk: how is he or she responding? Is this person beginning to see your point of view? Have you surprised your partner? As you talk, does he or she get angrier and angrier? Visualize the facial expressions and gestures—maybe your partner tries to interrupt you.

By concentrating so intensely on your imaginary partner, you achieve two things: you are truly and honestly reacting to another character (as you would in the play for which you're auditioning), and you are so deeply and thoroughly observing this imaginary person's responses that there is not enough room left in your mind to worry about everything that scares actors in the audition room.

Not *specifically* choosing who your character is talking to can ruin your entire monologue. It is not enough to say, "I/my character is talking to my ex-lover." You two have to have a history—just as you would in a real play. And your ex-lover has to have a face. Even if you're too nervous in the audition to see this face clearly, if you've seen this person in rehearsal you'll catch a glimpse of his or her face (or the outline of the body, or that silly hat he or she wears) while auditioning. That will give your acting focus and strength. Do whatever you need to do to personalize your imaginary scene partner. (If you use a person who is familiar to you in real life, your imaginary partner will be easier to see.) If you don't believe that the person you are talking to is present and in front of you, then how can the auditors?

Unfortunately, often an actor who has begun a monologue by seeing and fully relating to an imaginary partner will, after a few sentences, lose his or her commitment to the character he or she is talking to, and lose focus. Energy drops, concentration flags, and the actor delivers a so-so performance: a bad audition. You don't have to keep your eyes glued on your imaginary person at all times. But you *do* have to acknowledge his or her presence. Think about everyday-life conversations. We usually don't focus on people 100 percent of the time that we're talking to them. (That would probably be terribly unnerving for everyone involved!) But in an acting situation we need to heighten our focus a bit. Finding the right balance of focus in your monologue will be part of your work in rehearsal.

Ideally, your imaginary scene partner will be just a bit taller than you, so that when you look in this person's eyes, your face is clearly visible to the auditors. A slight change in the tilt of your head goes a long way in an audition. If you're talking to God or the heavens, raise your head just a *little* more; if you're talking to a child, don't make the child so short that you hide your face from the casting director.

In an audition situation it's best not to focus on more than one (or possibly two) imaginary characters. The more people you speak to in a monologue, the more chances you have of losing your focus and the specificity of your objectives and stakes. You're also more likely to cause your auditors to wonder where those imaginary characters are, distracting the auditors from your acting.

Sometimes monologues *are* written to be spoken to the masses: "Friends, Romans, countrymen, lend me your ears . . ." The trick here is to aim these speeches at individuals within the masses. If your monologue speaks to many people, be aware of them when you set up your environment. You can do this just before you begin your monologue by scanning "the crowd," so that the casting director knows they are there. After you have established your imaginary audience, keep your stakes and focus on one person (or maybe two). If you ask yourself, "Who am I talking to?" and your answer is, "Everybody," you have made a terrible acting choice and a huge audition mistake. Get more specific and focused by appealing to all but playing to one. Talk to everybody, but get your story to that one.

The one kind of audition piece in which you wouldn't have an imaginary scene partner is a soliloquy. Even then, if it's not a well-known soliloquy, you can successfully pretend you're talking to another character, rather than to yourself, making that character your imaginary partner.

The easiest way to "blow" a monologue audition is to gloss over your focus on the person you are supposed to be talking to, and to lose your commitment to your character and the environment you are existing in. It is not enough for you/your character to tell us the story; you must make us believe in the full environment of the present moment of that story.

WHERE TO LOOK

Should you use the auditor as the character you are talking to? As noted in Chapter 7 (under "Can You Look at Them?," page 49), individual casting people respond differently to this question. In an acting audition, most strongly prefer that you don't use them. And why would you want to? You've rehearsed carefully with an imaginary partner whose face and reactions you're familiar with. Why would you choose to audition instead with an unprepared (and quite possibly unwilling) scene partner? Let the auditor do his or her job—which is evaluating your performance, not ad-libbing his or her own—and you do yours.

Ideally, there will be about six feet between you and your auditor. The best place to put your imaginary scene partner is in that space, and one or two steps to your left or right. This way your monologue will have the same impact on the casting people as it does on your imaginary character, and you won't be auditioning in profile.

Cramped audition spaces—like agents' offices or tiny studios—are a special problem. I remember auditioning with a monologue in a room about the size of a broom closet; there was just about enough space for the casting director and her chair. She insisted that whatever I do, I not use her for the monologue, "Please do not look at me," she instructed. All I kept thinking was, "Where else *can* I look?" I took a breath, found my focus just past her shoulder, and performed one of the best auditions I have done in years—all in a room barely big enough to hold a mop and a bucket! In this particular situation, if I had put my imaginary scene partner "onstage" with me, I'd have been talking to a character just inches from my nose, and that would have diminished my performance.

DON'T LOOK DOWN

Looking down can disrupt the energy and focus of your piece in one quick second. I strongly suggest that you not do it unless it is a specific (and brief) choice.

Try reciting your monologue while looking down. What happens? All of your focus goes to the floor. Now, perform your monologue again, this time only looking down once in a while. What happened to the focus during those times? Again, it went to the floor. And where was your energy? Was it up and alive or was it mainly down and sluggish?

Think about your auditors. For two minutes they are going to (hopefully) give you their entire attention. If you look down for even a split second, so will they—and you'll lose their energy for several seconds more. Looking down is like telling a bad joke: its aftereffects linger on. Even the funny joke that follows won't be as funny as it should be, because your audience is still stuck in the mire of the bad one.

The other problem with looking down is that it is a clichéd and insecure choice; it's weak physically and it's weak emotionally. Looking down implies that you're not sure about a particular line or acting choice.

So before you insist, "But I need to look down!" test it. Try looking anywhere else when you need to look down. I find the more powerful choice for a look down is the *opposite*: look up (but not too far).

CHAPTER 16

Getting It Up on Its Feet

Now it's time to get your chosen monologue on its feet and begin the staging process. When you perform your pieces for auditions, you may find yourself in a room the size of a broom closet, standing only a couple of feet from your auditor; on a large stage with four or five casting people in the last row of the audience; or anywhere in between. You have to be ready for whatever challenges you might encounter, whether architectural or environmental (an open window, a noisy air conditioner, arpeggios in the adjacent studio . . .).

When you begin to rehearse your monologue, the first thing you want to do is give yourself an area of space in which to work: your "stage." Most monologues don't need a lot of space in performance, so your area doesn't have to be very big—about six feet square is ideal. Move the sofa against the wall in your living room and, voilà: your stage.

When you have chosen your acting area, treat it as if it actually *were* a stage. Place your imaginary audience about six feet in front of you. Designate center stage, upstage left, downstage right, etc. Step onto your stage and locate your imaginary scene partner. I like to use physical objects in the room to help me place my partner. For instance, if I am speaking to a character named Doris, I might choose a picture on the wall that would be at her eye level.

Make concrete decisions about your imaginary scene partner. Your choices should help clarify your monologue. If the character you are speaking to is a child or is in a wheelchair, establish height with your somewhat lowered focus. (Avoid standing while talking to a sitting character for more than a few seconds, though—the auditors won't be able to see your face.)

After you have mentally set up your stage and your scene partner, rehearse your monologue in the space. Feel free to move as you wish: upstage, downstage, left, right. Or choose not to move at all. When you have finished the monologue, note how your movement (or lack of movement) affected you.

After you have gone through your monologue a few times in the space, exploring different areas of your stage, take an accounting. Stop to think about what you did. The best choices you can make as you begin to block your monologue are those that make you (the actor, not necessarily the character) feel comfortable.

Next, knowing that there is no wrong answer to this question, ask yourself, "Where would I like to begin my monologue?" Where do your *instincts* tell you to begin? Upstage left, or right? Center stage, downstage?

Is your monologue slightly off-center and comedic, or dark and mysterious? In either of these situations, perhaps you should begin upstage left or right. That feeling of being away from center might help give you a better physical sense of your off-center character. Is your monologue straightforward, in-your-face? Then maybe begin center stage. Perhaps you want to start downstage center and end upstage center. Don't overanalyze or -intellectualize these decisions; just try using many combinations until the blocking feels right.

Always be aware of how your blocking will affect your audition in any given space. If you are very close to the casting director, for instance, a move from upstage center to downstage center can seem confrontational, and could make him or her uneasy. (Again, don't get any closer to an auditor than six feet during your monologue, unless a tiny space, like an office, forces you to.) This cross from upstage center to downstage center is very powerful and should be used appropriately—when you mean to show strength. Paradoxically, it can also be a vulnerable movement, if your character is acknowledging some kind of defeat. There are situations in which a character is confrontational in one moment, and vulnerable in the next. Physicalizing this tug-of-war can be fun.

I DIDN'T MOVE AT ALL

Did you explore your acting area and find that you just weren't comfortable moving, or that a particular cross didn't feel natural? Trust your instinct and don't push yourself. It's a good idea to show your auditors that you *can* move easily on a stage, but it doesn't take much movement to prove that (especially in a small space), and whatever you do should be motivated. Many actors are afraid to move in an audition; they'll sit in a chair and stay there, or they'll find their "mark" onstage and never leave it. You want to show the casting people that you're not one of these; but you also want to show them that you know how to use movement and gestures economically, in support of what you're saying—that you have control over your body.

There is never "nothing" onstage. You don't have to move to get the casting director's attention. If you are thoroughly invested in what you're saying—if your intentions, colors, stakes, and imaginary character are in place—this person will watch you standing still for a relatively long time ("long" can be thirty seconds in a two-minute audition). I refer to this as "active stillness," and it can be very powerful.

You will encounter many different audition spaces in your career. I have auditioned in a living room, a classroom, a hallway, a park, a hotel room, an opera house that seated thousands, and on and in all kinds of theater stages and studios. You won't be able to control where your audition takes place. But you can control *how you audition*. Practice your staging and be confident, so that when you encounter a strange space—and you will!—you can at least place your own stage area within that space.

CHAPTER 17

During the Audition

Okay . . . They are ready for you! This is it!

Remember that you are onstage—not in the wings—from the second you enter the audition room. Whatever you do from the instant you open the door will be seen and evaluated by the casting people. As you step into the room and acknowledge the auditors, also use that moment to scan the space and find your playing area. Every room has its unique trouble spots (an open window over a noisy street, awkward sight lines, a badly placed piano, etc.). Usually you can't fix them, but if you're aware of them before you start, you can probably work around them.

The monitor may have already given your photo and résumé to the auditors. If this hasn't been done, do that yourself when you greet them. They will probably say hello and ask what piece you'll be doing. On the other hand, they might say absolutely nothing. If they don't refer to you by name, introduce yourself (confidently), and then introduce your monologue—briefly. All you'll need to say are the title of the play and the names of the author and your character. If you have to explain your piece—or set it up in more than one *very* short sentence, then it is probably not a good choice for a monologue.

If your audition requires a chair, efficiently place it where you want it to be—you can do this as you introduce your piece. (Actors' Equity rules require that producers provide a chair in the audition room, but you can't count on having one at non-union calls.) Then place yourself.

The shift in your body and in your focus as you locate your imaginary scene partner cues the casting people that your audition has begun. Don't plunge into your lines; the auditors will welcome a moment of silence as they shift their thoughts from the previous actor's audition to yours. To imagine yourself into your monologue, use the "moment before" it begins. The "moment before" is your propulsion fuel—it propels you to speak.

Your imaginary scene partner helps you create your moment before. Is he or she speaking to you before you begin to talk? Do these lines prompt yours? Listen to your partner. Or, alternatively, are you initiating a conversation? Then you can use an internal monologue to put yourself into the scene. Internal monologues run through our heads in real life—we talk to ourselves, we plan things out, we evaluate.

Take, for instance, the monologue from *The Shadow Box* that was discussed in Chapter 14: Brian's first line is, "People don't want to let go. Do they?" If you were performing that in an audition, before you spoke you would locate and see the Interviewer, then either listen to a couple of lines that you've invented for him (what question did he just ask that compels your reply?) or run your own internal monologue. (What have you been thinking that leads you to realize, "people don't want to let go"?)

Listening—either to your imaginary partner or to your own words in your head—will help you see the character to whom you're talking. And watching you listen will intrigue your auditors and draw them into your scene. You can rehearse these silent cues just as you do the spoken lines in your monologue.

You might also want to do some mental preparation before you enter the audition room, to help put yourself in your scene. This isn't the time for you to start a conversation with fellow actors. It's the time for you to focus and prepare for what is about to happen. While you're waiting to be called, begin imagining what happened in the moment before. Then see your monologue in front of you, visualizing the story as if it were scenes from a film. Now prepare to tell this story from beginning to middle to end. If you have been able to look into the audition room (or, better yet, have been able to get into it!), you can visualize yourself and your imaginary character performing in that specific space.

The more completely you can put yourself into the moment before, and the more clearly you can see your imaginary partner, the more likely it is that your concentration and your energy will be in the right place. You/your character will be focused on achieving your objective; your energy won't be sidetracked by anxiety.

FORGETTING LINES

If you are in the first few seconds of your monologue and you "go up"—forget your line—whether or not to start over is a judgment call. You will have to make that decision on the spot. Casting people see actors lose their lines frequently, and they know it's a normal response to a high-anxiety situation. I don't think there is anything wrong with beginning again if you have just begun the piece. You can simply tell the casting director, "Sorry, false start," and begin a second time. Or say something like, "I am going to begin again," or "I am going to start the monologue over." Don't be too apologetic about going up; just acknowledge it quickly and get on with your performance! Remember: casting directors are human, too, and mistakes happen.

If you are more than a few lines into your monologue and you go blank, do not start over. One thing to try is this: take a breath, slow down, calm yourself, and simply repeat the last line you said, with the same commitment. You have just bought yourself some precious time to get back to the text. I have seen this trick done often with monologues that I know every word of, and the only time it doesn't work is when the actor stumbles or loses focus. If you're confident in your delivery, the auditor could think that you decided to repeat the line for emphasis. Make a fully committed choice—keep the flow going; stay on the roller coaster.

For the long run of your monologue, a better choice when you go blank is not to repeat your last line, but to keep on going: ad-lib it. If you forget what you're supposed to say—"I'm starved; I would really love a thick cheeseburger and fries right now"—it's perfectly fine to ad-lib, "I'm really hungry; I'd like something to eat."

The first thing that stage fright takes away is your memorization. But forgetting your line doesn't mean that you've forgotten why you're saying it, or what you're trying to accomplish. Trust yourself to continue to pursue your goal with different words. Paraphrase. Let your motivation carry you. You'll soon find your way back to what you've memorized; and the casting director either won't know that you went up, or will be impressed by your recovery. Using this approach gives you confidence and makes it less likely that you'll lose the same line again under pressure.

It is important to acknowledge that in live performance, there is always, always, the possibility that things can go wrong. A good auditor knows this and judges accordingly. It's your job to come in well prepared, to be in control of what you *can* control, and to respond professionally to what you can't.

FINISHING UP

As you near the end of your monologue, don't be in a rush to leave the room. Don't show us that the end of your performance is coming before you have even finished speaking. Keep watching your imaginary scene partner—how is he or she reacting to what you're saying? Your focus and energy won't slip at the end of your monologue if your character still needs to know (or hope) that his or her goal has been accomplished.

Don't race through your last few words; let them "play out." When you've finished speaking, you're still performing. Let your monologue linger in the air for a moment, like the final note in a piano concerto. Hold your auditors for a couple of beats with the energy of your silence and expectation—you're still watching your scene partner. Then simply break out of your scene. One way to do that is to slightly readjust your body, take a good breath, exhale, and switch your focus to the casting people. Look the primary auditor (e.g., the casting director, not his assistant) in the eye and say, "Thank you," then efficiently leave the room.

Sometimes—for reasons big or small, justified or silly—you'll feel that your audition wasn't up to par. *Never* comment on the quality of your audition to the casting people, either verbally or with your body language. Don't apologize for what could be imagined "mistakes." Leave the room like a professional who has completed his job. You are, and you have.

REVIEW: AUDITION ESSENTIALS

The following items provide a handy checklist of audition essentials:

1. Know the title of the play, etc. that your monologue is from.

2. Know who wrote it.

3. Know who your imaginary scene partner is.

4. As you enter the room, find your staging area.

5. See your imaginary scene partner before you begin your monologue.

6. When you finish your monologue, let your last note play out.

7. Say, "Thank You."

8. Be prepared with at least two other monologues. (They may want to see more.)

Also see "Ten Pitfalls," in Chapter 5, "Before the Audition," page 35.

CHAPTER 18

Exploration Exercises

The twenty-seven exercises below are included to help you explore each of your monologues in every way possible, and to freshen up a monologue that's begun to feel stale or boring. They can also be used for your song explorations.

The exercises come from many different sources. Some I've learned from teachers I've worked with over the years; some are just "in the air"; and some are my own, or are variations on other people's ideas. They can be explored alone, but are better if done with a partner or in a group. Probably every one of your monologues would benefit from every one of these exercises, but that doesn't mean you "have" to use all of them before auditioning with your piece. They're listed in no particular order. Play around with them; you'll be surprised at the different insights and approaches you discover.

PROOFREADING
Purpose: to review your memorization
Sit in a comfortable position with your spine aligned. Look at your text. Now, starting at the top, focus on one line or sentence. Memorize it word-for-word including the punctuation. Look away from the text (or look at your partner) and say the line you just read. Go through the entire monologue this way. This is an excellent tool to get you reacquainted with the text and reaffirm your confidence in having the words fully memorized and the energy flowing.

LIFE OR DEATH
Purpose: to help raise the stakes
Go through the entire monologue (fully memorized) while saying it as if doing so meant life or death. Treat it as if there were nothing more important in the world at this very moment than what you have to say right now.

JUST THE FACTS
Purpose: to help find the different acting colors
Now try the monologue as if you were giving a very boring factual lecture. Don't try to put any "acting" on this; just deliver the facts, almost in a monotone.

THE SEDUCTION
Purpose: to help find the different acting colors

Perform your monologue as if everything you were doing was for the sole purpose of seducing someone.

SO FUNNY
Purpose: to help find the different acting colors
Everything you say is the funniest thing on earth; nothing is funnier. Every word, every sentence, every thought is filled with so much laughter you cannot breathe. (This exercise works wonderfully for serious dramatic pieces. Trust this: you can find moments of humor in the most serious pieces—and you might decide to use those moments in your monologue. Think of people who laugh out of nervousness when they are given serious news.)

SO SAD
Purpose: to help find the different acting colors
The opposite of "So Funny." Everything you have to say is the saddest. Take it as far as you can. Explore all levels of sad.

CAVE PEOPLE/LIGHTHOUSE
Purpose: to help find the important words in your text that may need emphasis
Go through your entire monologue and cross out any words that are not important. Don't be stingy! Really ask yourself if you need a word. If not, cross it out. Chances are you don't need as many words as you think.

Then perform your "new" monologue with only those essential words. *At first* the text will sound like cave-people talk, but after a few performances, you will have replaced the unnecessary words with your own acting and subtext. Hopefully, you will come to rely more on your physical, vocal, and subtextual world, and less on the actual text.

Think of those absolutely necessary words that you are reciting and performing as "lighthouse words." On a foggy night a boat can navigate its way to shore aided by the beam from a lighthouse. Similarly, you can rely on the lighthouse words that you have chosen to keep you safely on course.

NOUN EMPHASIS
Speak only the nouns.

VERB EMPHASIS
Speak only the verbs.

ADJECTIVE EMPHASIS
(You guessed it!) Speak only the adjectives.

VOWEL EMPHASIS

Using the vowels of your text as your only text, explore the vowels and their weight without the consonants. Try connecting the vowels, inflecting the vowels, chanting the vowels. Take note of the differences you experience throughout the text.

CONSONANT EMPHASIS

Same as above, but with consonants.

WHISPER

Speak through the text in a whisper. It is important not to put too much stress on the physical act of whispering. Rather, the whisper should feel effortless and unforced.

SMALL, MEDIUM, LARGE

Explore the text vocally, using different levels of volume. (If you are working with a partner, have the partner suggest a volume by calling out at random times, "small," "medium," or "large.")

FAST

Purpose: to wrap your tongue around the words and to build confidence
See if you can speed through the piece vocally and speak as much of the monologue as possible in one minute.

PAUSE

Purpose: to find the natural pauses in your monologue
Count to ten in your head before you speak *each* line. During these ten-second moments you must keep the monologue alive by justifying a reason for the pause. When you have completed this exercise, mark down where a pause might be a good choice.

CHANGE

Purpose: to identify and feel when a change has occurred
While reciting the monologue, any time you feel a change occur—physical, emotional, or vocal—acknowledge the change by saying out loud, "Change." Mark the moments of change and use them in your monologue to deepen your choices.

Note: In a two-minute monologue, it is very possible that you can have 100 or more changes! *If at any time a change occurs, no matter how small—even if it is only your taking a breath—you must acknowledge it as a change.*

MATCHSTICK

(Make sure you don't burn yourself or your surroundings!) Try this exercise with a wooden match. Light the match and see if you can get through your entire monologue before the match burns your fingers. The exercise will instill the sense of urgency that comes with high stakes. It also may show you where you can speed up the slow parts of your monologue.

GOOD FOR ME/BAD FOR ME

Purpose: to identify specific moments and how you/the character feels about each one
While performing the monologue, when you find moments that are good for you, say out loud, "Good"; when they are bad for you, say out loud, "Bad." There should never be an "I'm not sure" moment.

SILENT

Purpose: to identify and emphasize your physical actions
Perform the monologue as you would usually—except without words. Try to communicate as much of your monologue as you did when you were speaking it. This works well for songs, too.

SONG DROP-IN

Purpose: to help you get started with your monologue
You can actually do this in your head moments before you perform it in your audition. Pick a song or melody that your character from the monologue would choose to sing or hum to comfort him- or herself. Sing or hum through it; when you feel ready to begin your monologue, use that music in your head to transition you into your piece seamlessly.

PARAPHRASE

Put the monologue into your own words—how you would really say it.

THREE CHAIRS

Purpose: to find the beat changes
Set up three chairs in a row, next to each other. Begin your monologue seated on one chair. When you feel a beat change, move to the next chair, and then the next. Keep going, using the same three chairs, until you feel you have exhausted *all* of the beat changes or have finished the monologue.

I'M BORED

(This idea is based on an exercise from Keith Johnstone's *Impro for Storytellers*. It is an excellent exercise to test how effectively you are engaging the audience.)

Perform your monologue in front of a few people. Advise the people watching to actually leave the room if they are no longer interested in you and your monologue. Your job is to keep them in the room! If even one person leaves, you must identify and acknowledge why he or she left. (A sometimes-difficult exercise, but important in finding the weak spots in your monologue.)

SING YOUR MONOLOGUE

Simply sing through your entire monologue as if it were a song. This is a good exercise to help loosen you up. You may also find some nice vocal moments that you haven't explored before.

SONG AND DANCE

Now treat your monologue as if it were a song-and-dance number: sing and dance your way through it. This may help you find new ideas for blocking your piece, and give you more confidence in performing it.

BEHAVIORS

When you have "lived" with your monologue for a while and find that you are bored or stale, try this exercise. Perform your monologue and exhibit the following behaviors, in any order:

- fully extend body
- curl up into a small or fetal position
- cry
- laugh
- be still or silent
- run
- jump
- leap
- sing
- curse/call out to heaven, hell, or an "outside force"
- get mad enough to spit
- touch yourself

CHAPTER 19

Monologues to Avoid

Sometimes monologues from plays or movies become so popular that casting people are bored by them and would rather not see them performed again. Darren earlier mentioned a similar reaction to overdone songs (see "Overused Songs" in Chapter 1, page 18). Often this is cyclical: a rare monologue that you've used for years may suddenly become way too popular when the show it was taken from is revived on Broadway or released as a major motion picture. Ten years later everyone may have forgotten it. On the other hand, some monologues have been on the "overdone" list for decades: Laura's lines in *The Glass Menagerie*, or Starbuck's in *The Rainmaker*, for instance. It's hard to predict which monologues will remain overpopular, and which will fade away. That's why you're always better off when you take the time and make the effort to find out-of-the-way selections. When you walk into the audition room with a piece that the auditors haven't heard of, you're already a little bit ahead of the game.

Passages from the following plays were being excerpted so often for audition monologues in 2005 that I urge you not to use them:

CONTEMPORARY MONOLOGUES

A . . . My Name Is Alice
Agnes of God
Album
All My Sons
Angels in America
True West
Boy's Life
Bums
Butterflies Are free
Cat on a Hot Tin Roof
Crimes of the Heart
The Crucible
Death of a Salesman
The Effect of Gamma Rays on
　Man-in-the-Moon Marigolds
Fences
For Colored Girls Who Have Considered
　Suicide/When the Rainbow Is Enuf

The Glass Menagerie
Greater Tuna
I Hate Hamlet
Keely and Du
The Laramie Project
Laundry and Bourbon
Lone Star
Night Luster
Oleanna
Quilters
The Rainmaker
Rosencrantz and Guildenstern Are Dead
A Streetcar Named Desire
Where Has Tommy Flowers Gone?
Wit
The Woolgatherer
Anything by Neil Simon
Anything by Christopher Durang
Anything by Eric Bogosian

CLASSICAL MONOLOGUES—MEN

Sophocles
Creon, *Antigone*

Shakespeare
Angelo, *Measure for Measure*
Benedick, *Much Ado about Nothing*
Bottom, *A Midsummer Night's Dream*
Brutus, *Julius Caesar*
Chorus, *Henry V* (The opening speech,
  "O for a muse of fire . . .," is overdone
  by men and women.)
Hamlet, *Hamlet* (All of his lines are
  overdone by men and women.)
Henry, *Henry V*
Hotspur, *Henry IV, Part* 1
Iago, *Othello*
Launcelot Gobbo, *The Merchant of Venice*
Puck, *A Midsummer Night's Dream*
Oberon, *A Midsummer Night's Dream*
Orsino, *Twelfth Night*
Petruchio, *The Taming of the Shrew*
Shylock, *The Merchant of Venice*

Christopher Marlowe
Faustus, *Dr. Faustus*

Molière
Tartuffe, *Tartuffe*

Edmond Rostand
Cyrano, *Cyrano de Bergerac*

CLASSICAL MONOLOGUES—WOMEN

Euripides
All roles in *Medea*
All roles in *The Trojan Women*

Sophocles
Antigone, *Antigone*

Aristophanes
All roles in *Lysistrata*

Shakespeare
Lady Macbeth, *Macbeth*
Juliet, *Romeo and Juliet*
Phebe, *As You Like It*
Portia, *The Merchant of Venice*
Ophelia, *Hamlet*
Helena, *A Midsummer Night's Dream*

Molière
Célimène, *The Misanthrope*

Racine
Phaedra, Oenone, *Phaedra*

Oscar Wilde
All roles in *The Importance of Being Earnest*

George Bernard Shaw
Barbara, *Major Barbara*

PART THREE

Practical Information for Actors

CHAPTER 20

Résumés

Your photo and résumé—stapled together at all four corners—are your "calling card" as an actor. More often than not, they are the casting person's first glimpse of you. Your photo-résumé should be an honest, professional, and current representation of who you are. Your résumé lists for the auditors your representative credits and experience, and gives them something tangible to take away from your audition and keep on file.

Samples of two résumés appear on the following pages. They're laid out in a simple, fairly standard format. Look at other actors' résumés, too, though, as you advance in your career; you may want to vary your layout somewhat. Warning: don't get *too* creative. If the casting people can't read your résumé easily, they may not bother to read it at all.

RÉSUMÉ BASICS

Length
Your acting résumé should not exceed one page. As your career advances and you accumulate more credits, keep moving the lesser ones to the bottom until eventually they are eliminated. Only designers, directors, choreographers, and musical directors can sometimes use more than one page, because they are applying for staff or administrative positions.

Color
Résumés should be printed on white paper. Résumés printed on colored paper suggest that the actor is desperate to be noticed; this makes me a bit leery. A well-prepared audition will get you the role, not a colorful résumé.

Dimensions
Résumés are usually typeset on standard 8" x 11" paper. However, because you will be stapling your résumé to the back of your 8" x 10" photo, don't set the margins too close to *any* edge, or you'll risk losing some copy when trimming the paper.

RÉSUMÉ CONTENT

Name
Your name should always be at the top center of your résumé. It should be typeset in boldface type. Be proud of it.

AUDITION JOE
(212) 555-5555

Height: 6'0"   Hair: Brown   Eyes: Hazel   Voice: Tenor

Community Theater
Fiddler on the Roof	Perchik	Long Island Players
Grease	Danny	Plainview Dinner Theater
Damn Yankees	Ensemble	Bradford Road Theater Co.
Arsenic and Old Lace	Mr. Gibbs	Rembrandt PlayhouseTheater

Vocal Experience
All-State Choir	Tenor	New York State
Madrigal Singers	Tenor	JFK High School
Show Choir	Soloist	JFK High School

Educational Theater
Oklahoma!	Curley	NYU
Anything Goes	Ensemble	NYU
42nd Street	Featured Dancer	NYU

Training
NYU Theater Major
JFK High School
Voice: P. C. Epstein
Acting: Ryan Drew
Dance: Allie Nicole

Special Skills
Southern accent, gymnastics, jazz singing, juggling, piano (eight years).

Sample beginner's résumé

AUDITION JOE
AEA — SAG
(212) 555-5555

Height: 6'0"   Hair: Brown   Eyes: Hazel   Voice: Tenor

Broadway
Wicked	Ensemble	Gershwin Theatre
A Chorus Line	Paul	Shubert Theatre
42nd Street	Billy	Majestic Theatre
Me and My Girl	Ensemble	Marquis Theatre

Off-Broadway
Little Shop of Horrors	Seymour	Orpheum Theatre
The Fantasticks	Matt	Sullivan St. Playhouse

Regional
Footloose	Ren	Sacramento Music Circus
Zorba	Dancer	North Shore Music Theatre

Television
Law & Order	Lawyer	NBC
Third Watch	Fireman	NBC
Frasier	Waiter	NBC

Commercials
Conflicts available upon request

Film
Two Weeks Notice	Taxi driver
Spiderman	Crossing Guard

Dialects
Standard British, German, French, Southeastern United States.

Special Skills
Jazz scatting, gymnastics, cheerleading, martial arts, hip-hop dancing.

Sample professional performer's résumé

Home Address

I advise you *not* to put your home address on your résumé. This is especially important if you are sending a picture and résumé through the mail in response to a casting notice, with no knowledge of who is seeing them. Your residence is private information that should remain private. There is no reason to divulge it until a producer is ready to mail you a contract.

Telephone Number

For the same reason, I suggest not putting your home telephone number on your résumé. You should invest in an answering service, cell phone, or pager. If you are performing on the road and a theater calls you about an audition, you cannot count on your roommates at home to relay the message to you; and if your answering machine is not functioning properly, you can miss a callback. With your own personal number, the industry can always reach you. It would be a crime to spend years networking and promoting your career, only to become unfindable because you have moved or are working out of town.

E-mail Address

Many agencies and casting directors are now using e-mail for correspondence, so having your e-mail address on your résumé is very helpful.

Union affiliation

Once you become a member of any professional actors union, you are expected to list it on your résumé—usually right below your name. The three major actors unions are Actors Equity Association (AEA), the Screen Actors Guild (SAG), and the American Federation of Television and Radio Artists (AFTRA).

Representation

If you are represented by an agency or management company, you need to list its name, address, and contact numbers on your résumé. Very often, the agency that represents you will print that information on adhesive labels that you can put at the top of your résumé.

Age

There is no need to include your age on your résumé. However right you may be for a particular role, once a director discovers that you are actually ten years older than the character, he or she may suddenly become biased. At an Equity audition the panelists are not allowed to ask your age. If you are asked but don't want to tell them your actual age, a suggested response is, "Onstage I usually read between . . ." or, "I am as old or as young as you would like me to be." The auditors should take the hint.

When I was casting a show called *Sally Blane—Teenage Girl Detective*, loosely based on the Nancy Drew mysteries, Sally's character needed to be around seventeen years old. The casting director brought in a mix of real seventeen and eighteen year olds, and twenty-five year olds who looked about seventeen. He refused to tell the director and me which was which, so that our decision would be based on talent, rather than actual age. We wound up casting a twenty-five year old simply because she was the best actress and singer.

To be honest, if I had known the actress's true age, I might not have selected her.

Height

Having height on your résumé is very helpful when the panel is trying to pair up couples after you have left. For instance, if you are being considered for a leading role, the auditors need to know that your height is 5' 2", in case the person they are considering to play opposite you is 6' 2". Auditors must weigh so many details when casting; don't make them guess at your height.

Hair Color

Listing your hair color is helpful, but not as important as stating your height. Wigs are so often used onstage, especially in a period piece, that the true color of your hair almost doesn't matter. If the role you are auditioning for does require a certain hair color, and the theater is not using wigs, then the auditors might ask if you would be willing to change your hair color for the show. Still, during the actual casting process, knowing the color of your hair can help the panelists remember you. For example, "I'm not sure which singer you're talking about; I've seen so many good ones today. . . . Oh, you mean the one with the big voice and the long, blonde hair."

Eye Color

The color of your eyes can't be seen by most of the audience, especially in a large theater. Eye color matters, however, when casting for television or film, because close-up camera shots reveal all the subtleties of your features.

Weight

Listing your weight on your résumé, although appropriate for film, commercial, and television auditions, is not necessary for a theater audition.

Voice Range

If your voice is still very young and changing all the time, it is not necessary to specify your exact vocal range. Until you feel that your voice has settled into a consistent range, I would suggest listing your voice type: for example, soprano/belt, baritone, alto, bari/tenor, or mezzo-soprano.

If you are asked your vocal range, you must have an accurate answer. Women who have a belt/chest voice and a soprano/head voice should make sure they know the range of each.

Don't give an answer or print anything on your résumé that you cannot follow through on, and don't guess what your high note is. In determining your range, remember that it can be altered by your adrenaline level when you are actually performing for an audience. Your range must be the territory between the extreme notes you can call upon at any time of the day and those under any level of stress, regardless of the weather and your mood. Telling a musical director that you normally have a high B flat in your range—it's just not there today—will not help you. He or she needs to hear it now; you cannot expect to be called back or hired on blind faith.

If someone on the panel is *truly* interested in you, but your material hasn't shown enough range and you don't know your range, the musical director will vocalize you at the audition—but this shouldn't be necessary.

Commercials

If you include a category for commercials on your résumé, instead of listing each product that you advertised, you should simply write, "Conflicts available upon request." Why? Because, for example, if you've filmed a commercial for Pepsi, the producer of a Coke commercial probably won't hire you. To do so would create a conflict of interest. Even if your contractual commitment for Pepsi has terminated, Coke might not want to use an actor who once promoted its competitor.

RÉSUMÉ FORMATTING

Although there are several acceptable ways to lay out your résumé, the most common and easiest to read is the three-column format used in the examples on pages 120–121. In this format, subject headings are followed by specific information arranged in—yes—three columns.

One way to list your credits would be in this order: Stage, Theater, Film, Television, Commercials; Training (teachers); Education (school); and any Special Skills that may interest the audition panel. A list of such categories is on pages 120–121.

Here are three examples of formatting options for your résumé's heading. If you want to design yours differently, that's fine, but don't get too fancy. Your heading needs to be very clear and easy for the reader to follow.

Catagorizing Credits: Some Headings

You can pick and choose from among the following suggestions:

- Broadway

- National Tours

- European Tours

Heading Option #1

AUDITION JOE

Telephone number

Height:

Weight:

Hair Color:

Voice Type:

.

Heading Option #2 (using a box)

AUDITION JOE

Telephone number

E-mail Address

Height:	Hair:	Voice Type:	Eyes:

Heading Option #3 (using underlining)

AUDITION JOE

E-mail Address

Telephone number

Voice Type:

Hair:

Eyes:

Height:

- Off-Broadway

- Regional Theater

- Summer Stock

- Dinner Theater

- Community Theater

- Educational Theater (High School, College)

- Revues/Theme Parks/Cruise Ships

- Television

- Film

- Commercials

- Vocal Experience (e.g., All-State Choir, A Cappella Singing Group)

- Education, Training

- Dialects

- Special Skills

Listing Credits

It is common to list your credits in order of importance, rather than chronologically. A leading role that you performed a year ago still holds more clout than a chorus part in a show you just completed.

New York City casting directors usually want to see stage credits first, whereas Los Angeles casting directors want to see film and television credits first. Some casting directors suggest that bicoastal actors have two résumés prepared—one for New York and regional theater work, one for Los Angeles.

At a busy audition, assume the panel will only have time to glance at the top third of your résumé. Therefore, list all of your important credits first, including leading roles and noteworthy theaters.

Name-Dropping

Listing directors' names next to each show is not necessary, unless a given director is very well known throughout the industry. Most likely your local dance teacher will make no impression on anyone in the professional world.

Job Location

When listing a theater that you performed in, note its location by either the state or the nearest large city. This validates the credit, and if someone on the panel happens to know the area, it can start a conversation. Any conversation gives the panel a sense of your personality.

Understudying

If you have understudied a role, you can write it on your résumé in one of two ways. If you understudied but never performed the role, it is proper to write "name of role u/s." If you understudied and *did* perform the role—Tony in *West Side Story*, for instance—the credit should be written as "Tony u/s (performed)." If you were also in the ensemble, write "Ensemble/Tony (u/s)." This is correct whether you have or have not gone on as Tony.

School Credits

Do not feel uncomfortable about using high school, college, or community theater credits on your résumé when you are first starting out. We all have to start somewhere, so be proud of your accomplishments. If you are twenty-one years old, how many—if any—professional credits can the panel expect you to have?

Other Credits You Can Include When First Starting Out

These may prove to be useful for your early jobs:

- Choral festivals and awards (these tell the musical director that you have experience in harmony singing)

- Pageants

- A cappella singing groups (these suggest that you have a good musical ear)

- Scholarships to schools, or to performing arts camps or festivals

- Master classes with notable artists

- Cruise ships and theme parks

- High school band and orchestra (these tell the musical director that you have some skill in reading music)

Nonperformance Credits: Special Skills

Technical skills, painting skills, and sewing/costume skills are all very valuable assets. Most non-Equity summer stock companies require you to have a certain number of these abilities. They should be listed collectively under the heading "Special Skills," rather than each having a separate header. Remember, this is an actor's *performance* résumé.

Listing special skills at the bottom of your résumé gives the auditors more insight into who you are. Special skills can run the gamut from impressions or whistling to the ability to read music or play an instrument to juggling or roller-skating. Don't forget the more mundane "skills," either; sometimes, especially in film or TV, casting directors need an actor who can drive a car or smoke a cigarette. Sometimes a director will add your skills to a character to make him or her more interesting.

Be able to follow through if asked to demonstrate any of your listed skills—unless, of course, a prop is involved. You certainly aren't expected to walk around with a trumpet or a pair of stilts in your bag. However, if the panel is interested in your skills as a trumpeter or a stilt walker, you will probably be asked to return at a later date with your trumpet or stilts. Don't list skills that you can barely pull off. Casting directors expect a certain level of proficiency—if "ice skating" is on your résumé, you'd better be able to do more than wobble around the rink.

References

When you list the names of people you trained with, it's often assumed that they can be used as references. If you have studied with someone who possibly won't remember you, or whom you didn't get along with, you might want to consider omitting his or her name.

If the casting people are interested in hiring you, they may look at your résumé hoping to recognize the name of someone you studied with, so they can contact him or her for a personal and professional reference.

To prevent any misunderstanding as to who your references are, I suggest writing "References Upon Request" at the bottom of your résumé. Keep a separate list with the names of your references, their telephone numbers, and their connection to the business. To make sure that a "recommendation" doesn't backfire on you, you should always ask your references ahead of time whether they feel comfortable about recommending you.

For example, Allie, a student of mine from several years ago, was being considered for a leading role in a musical. I received a call from the producer telling me that Allie had listed me as a reference, but I remembered her name and little else. I offered to look through old paperwork, for any comments I might have written down about her talent and work ethic. Allie was lucky: if I had been on the road without access to my files, I would not have been able to give the recommendation she needed. After reading through some old papers, I did remember her, and she got the job.

It's important to add that, yes, Allie had asked my permission to use me as a reference, but it had been so many years (and about a thousand students) ago, that I simply couldn't remember her well enough to give an honest reference. It would have helped if she had called me before her audition—to refresh my memory.

Updating

Keep your résumé neat and easy to read. Don't have more than one or two handwritten changes/updates. Nowadays, almost everyone has access to a computer, so there are no excuses anymore for not updating your résumé as needed.

Fabricated credits

Do *not* make up credits. This is such a small business that the odds are good you will get caught.

At one time, I worked for a producer who owned two theaters in different parts of the country. During auditions for one of those theaters, an actor walked in with credits stating that he had performed in three shows at the other venue. The producer had no idea who this actor was and confronted him. To make a long story short, a very embarrassed actor exited the room, having learned an important lesson about lying.

CHAPTER 21

Headshots

A headshot stapled to the back of your résumé is essential for any audition. The panel members will need to refer to your photo when casting, long after you've left the room. They cannot possibly remember what scores of people looked like, much less match names and faces from memory.

ESSENCE

The headshot needs to look like the actor looks when walking into the audition. Virtually any casting person interviewed on the subject will tell you that this is your photo's most important job. A headshot must also capture the essence of who you are. I prefer to see a picture of a smiling actor—someone who looks friendly and easy to work with—but there are casting people who say they dislike "seeing teeth."

The eyes are the most communicative feature in a headshot. They should be expressive and natural—and they should not be upstaged by your outfit, excessive jewelry or makeup, "artistic" lighting, or a distracting background. Also, a blank and posed stare doesn't convey much to a casting director—there's no life in it, and no hint of the individual behind the eyes. Pictures for theater auditions should not be modeling or glamour shots; casting people want to see a mind and personality, not just an attractive face and figure.

If your look or appearance drastically changes, you'll need new headshots that reflect the new you. Aging, a major loss or gain of weight, a change in the color or length of hair, or changes in a man's facial hair—any of these changes can alter your look so much that your auditors won't recognize you from your photo. If you and your picture don't look alike, your picture is useless.

FINDING THE RIGHT PHOTOGRAPHER

The best way to find the "right" photographer for you is to look at other actors' headshots and see which ones pique your interest. Ask yourself what appeals to you about another actor's picture—and ask yourself whether that quality would attract and inform a casting person. Has the photographer captured the actor's persona, and the light in his or her eyes? Do the tone, the lighting, the physical background, the pose, and/or the photographer's style support the image of the actor—or do they distract from the face?

You *must* take the time to research different photographers. View their work. Call them to find out their price ranges. Once you've narrowed down your prospects to half a dozen or so people, make appointments to visit their studios in person. Look through their portfolios to get a sense of their styles and tastes. Talk to each photographer to get a sense of how he or she works. This step is crucial. Getting to know a photographer as much as you can *before* your shoot will help you to relax *during* your shoot. Actors tend to overlook the fact that the photo session can be very stressful.

Some other details to ask about: how many rolls of film does the photographer use? Does he or she shoot in black-and-white film only, or in color? (Traditionally, the standard theater photo is shot in black and white, although color photos have been creeping in on both coasts—especially in California.) Do you get to keep the negatives? (This rarely happens.) How soon can you get the contact sheets back, and may you keep them? (Contact sheets show postage-stamp-size versions of all shots taken. These are printed directly off the negatives. Since they haven't been blown up, they're best viewed with a "loupe," which is similar to a magnifying glass.) If you are unhappy with your pictures, will the photographer do another shoot or a partial shoot at no extra charge?

Many photographers advertise their services in trade papers like *Back Stage* in the New York area, *Back Stage West* around Los Angeles, and *PerformInk* in Chicago. Most photography studios in New York City have their own Web sites, which list their costs and policies, as well as offer slide shows of their portfolios. So far, the best site that I have found is www.reproductions.com, which links you to hundreds of photography Web sites in New York and Los Angeles.

If you're in a smaller theater city, you may need to look harder for photographers who specialize in actors' headshots; here's another case where surfing the Web and networking with fellow performers pays off. If you're in a small town and just starting out, you can probably get a serviceable theater picture from a local photographer—especially if you show this person some samples of good actors' headshots on the Web or in the trades, and can clearly state your priorities. But when you move on in your career, and into a theater city, you'll need to find a specialist who knows what casting people expect to see.

ATTIRE

Bring several changes of clothing to the photo session. You might want to bring a variety of styles—formal, casual, sporty, business, preppie, etc.—but stay away from clothes that make you feel uncomfortable. Talk to your photographer in advance about what colors, patterns, and styles to avoid.

COST

Quality headshots don't come cheap, but they are an investment that should last you for several years. Because they are usually your important introduction to a casting person, don't cut corners here. Although an expensive photographer is not necessarily a good one, a beginner who is a "bargain" can be an expensive mistake. The cost of having your headshots taken in New York City can range from $200.00 to over $1,000.00. This excludes the costs of makeup, hairstyling, "touch-ups," and reprints.

Some photographers welcome you and a friend to share a session. This means that each of you will pay half price, and will get half of the total shots taken.

TYPES OF HEADSHOTS

The most common and preferred type of theatrical headshot is a picture of your face from the neck up—that's why they're called headshots. As the industry changes and time passes, different trends come and go. The three-quarter shot, for example, includes your upper body as well as your face. This style remains very popular.

Full-body shots are also common, and are useful in several situations. A commercial agent, for example, receives daily casting breakdowns for very specific physical types. If you happen to be in an agent's files, but this person doesn't know you very well, he or she can look at your three-quarter or full-body shot while deciding whether you are "right" to submit. Also, when a casting director posts a casting notice in the trade papers, requesting headshot-résumé submissions by mail, this person won't know many of the respondents. Again, seeing their body types will help him or her to decide how suitable they are for the project. The drawback of full and three-quarter shots is that as the camera backs off to catch more of your body, your face—and your expressive eyes—become smaller.

Some casting people recommend that actors have different shots for commercial, legit stage/film, and soap opera work. Commercial shots tend to be upbeat and smiley, theater shots more neutral, and soap shots more sexy. If you want to start out with just one photo, an appealing, direct look is probably best. These are broad generalizations, though, and you should think about what you want to convey (and to whom) before your shoot. In any case, remember: the person in the photo has to look like you will look when you walk into the audition room.

CHOOSING THE RIGHT SHOT

Ask friends and colleagues for their opinions on which shots capture you best, as it is not easy to be completely objective about yourself. Leave the room while they look at your contact sheets, so that your preferences don't influence their choices. Make a note of everyone's opinions, and take time to keep looking over the contacts until you have narrowed down your search to two shots. (Usually photographers give you two free 8" x 10" blowups from your contact sheets.) If you'll only be using one photo when job hunting, select it from these two "finalists."

COPIES/REPRODUCTIONS

Now that you have chosen which 8" x 10" photo (or photos) you'll be using, it is your job to take it to a reproduction lab. There a negative is created from your headshot, and from that negative are printed as many copies as you need and want to pay for. Actors usually begin with 100 copies.

Most actors have their names printed at the bottom of their headshots. This is a good idea because it helps directors and casting directors know who you are without having to turn the picture over to read your résumé. Reproduction labs do this printing for a small extra charge.

"TOUCH-UPS"

Many labs can "touch up," "cover up," or delete unwanted facial hair and blemishes. The purpose of retouching is to clean up unwanted details, *not* to create a new person. The best candidates for retouching are *nonpermanent* features: temporary blemishes, under-eye bags or shadows from lack of sleep, wrinkles emphasized by harsh studio lighting, shadows from the shoot, etc.

PHOTO POSTCARDS AND "COMPOSITES"

Postcards serve as a great "follow-up" when doing mailings to agents and casting directors. There is no need to send them the same 8" x 10" and résumé over and over again (unless you have gotten new pictures or have changed your contact information).

Some actors display two different looks on their postcards: a man may have facial hair on one shot and be clean shaven on the other; he might show his naturally balding head in one picture and wear a hairpiece in the second; and a woman who regularly wears glasses could use them in one photo and wear contact lenses in the other. The expense of reproducing postcards about equals that of duplicating 8" x 10"s.

"Composites" are 8" x 10"s or postcards showing multiple photos and looks. With the exception of the two-shot postcards just described, composites are not used in the theater. They are used for modeling and print work.

DIGITAL PHOTOGRAPHY

More and more headshot photographers are "going digital," which means that you can view your shots immediately after they are taken. Any retouching required can be done right in the studio while you watch. Ask different photographers about the pros and cons of a digital shoot as compared with the conventional method.

IN CONCLUSION

This chapter merely outlines the headshot process. For detailed information, head to your local theater bookstore for a full-length guide, or watch for the feature article that runs annually in *Back Stage* and *Back Stage West*.

CHAPTER 22

Getting Experience

When first starting out, you should focus on getting as much experience as possible. There is much to be learned—positive and negative—that is never taught in school. Start meeting and networking with other actors; begin to discover how different directors work, and how their approaches differ. You need to learn the *business* aspect of "show business" as much as you need to study your craft. Too many performers are taken advantage of because they lack business smarts.

WORK IS WORK

If you have based yourself in a major theater city, but are offered a show at a reputable theater out of town, you should definitely consider taking the job. Aside from the working experience itself, an out-of-town job offers such benefits as traveling the country for free and experiencing life on the road. Broaden your personal resources and life experiences. You will return a fuller person, which will make you a fuller actor—and exploring another city while getting paid isn't such a bad thing.

One July I ran into a very talented former student of mine, and asked him why he wasn't performing in a summer stock company somewhere. He replied that a theater had cast him in several leading roles, but he had decided to stay in New York City for the summer—because he "didn't want to miss out on any auditions." I was appalled. A twenty-two-year-old actor with only college credits needs to be getting hands-on experience! Who would trust him with a role in a Broadway show, for instance, with no professional experience? Would you entrust a first-year medical student with your appendectomy?

Work is work! Go: learn your craft, wherever the job is. I recently came upon a quote that sums up the need for getting experience: "There is no such thing as luck. Luck is when opportunity meets preparedness."

NO, THANKS

Declining an offer from a producer who has just cast you in his or her show is a difficult and sensitive task. None of us wants to say, "no," even if we really don't want the job—because we are afraid that we'll burn bridges we very much want to leave standing. Responding with a couple of "no"s, no matter how much you actually want the job and want to work with the producer, is likely to turn him or her off in the future—because *no* one likes to be rejected, even producers. Remember: when you choose to attend an audition, the panelists have the right to assume that you want to be cast. The worst thing you can do is to lead them on by going to all of the callbacks knowing the entire time that you do not intend to accept an offer.

The best reason to turn down a job, of course, is that you have another acting job that perhaps pays more or will employ you for a much longer period of time. The worst reasons are, for instance, that you have vacation plans, your sister is in town during those weeks, or you thought it would be fun to try out new material at the audition. Most producers understand the financial woes of actors and the importance of being in a show that offers long-term employment.

If there *is* a job conflict, you must make clear that it arose very recently—so the producer doesn't assume that you have been stringing him or her along all this time. Here's an example of a legitimate conflict. Actors are constantly auditioning. When a performer has not received an offer from a producer after a few weeks, usually that performer can rightly assume that he or she was not cast. One dilemma that often arises is, after hearing nothing after Theatre One's callback, two months later you accept a job at Theater Two for a three-month contract. Just as you are about to return your signed contract for that show, the producer from Theater One—doing the show you really wanted, but thought you didn't get—calls to offer you the job because someone just dropped out—and Theater One's show comes with a year-long contract.

DECIDING WHETHER OR NOT TO ACCEPT AN OFFER

For most young actors just starting out, deciding whether or not to accept an offer to perform onstage in a show usually isn't difficult. You will have different priorities at various stages in your career, but the bottom line is to ask yourself, "What can I gain from this experience?" There are many factors to consider in making this decision. When I am offered a show as musical director or conductor, I use the following checklist to weigh the pros and cons:

1. What is the general reputation of the theater?

2. Is the director a working director who can lead to future jobs, or the producer who likes to direct?

3. What is the show? Have I done it three times already? Would I enjoy doing it again?

4. How long does the show run? Do I want to be out of town for that period of time?

5. Is this a theater that I would like to develop a working relationship with?

6. What is the salary? Can I afford it?

As an actor, you should also consider:

1. What role have you been offered? Is this your twentieth chorus part? If so, you may want to hold out for a better opportunity.

2. Is there a chance to understudy?

3. Does the theater offer Equity Membership Candidate credits?

4. Would taking this job give you your Equity card?

You have to decide whether the experience can become unpleasant and unproductive. If you feel that it might, then I suggest you decline an offer, instead of saying "yes" just because you feel that you "should."

SIGNING A CONTRACT

If an offer is made to you at the audition and you want to accept it, do so verbally, but never sign anything until you have taken the contract home and read it carefully. Check with knowledgeable friends and colleagues regarding any details you don't understand.

My first year out of college, I was offered a show with a six-month contract, for a considerable amount of money. I signed the contract, purchased new luggage, and received a phone call the next day from the producer, informing me that my services were no longer needed. In other words, I was fired. I found out later that the musical director who was originally offered the job had suddenly become available.

Ultimately, I hired a lawyer to battle the case. Because I had already signed the contract, my attorney believed that I had the right to be compensated. Well, guess what? I lost due to a technical error. The producer stated that I was in breach of contract *because I hadn't attended rehearsals.* He claimed that I should have shown up to work because the contract was signed.

Remember, I hadn't attended rehearsals *because I had been fired.* Still, the producers won their case based on the fact that I hadn't fulfilled my contractual obligation. If I had gone to the first day of rehearsal, the producer would have had to pay me.

This experience taught me an important lesson. I had thought that looking over a contract simply meant making sure that the salary, performance dates, and housing provisions agreed to in writing matched the offer that had been made to me verbally, over the phone. I had no knowledge of any legalities or "rights," because I had never signed a contract before—besides, what could go wrong? When I was fired I assumed there was nothing I could do (aside from pouting) but move on and continue to look for work. It wasn't until weeks later that a friend of mine told me I probably could have sued the producer for a breach of contract— but by then it was too late. If I had trusted the contract, and fulfilled my part of it by showing up at the first rehearsal, then I probably could have fought for severance pay. Or if I had contacted a lawyer immediately, I could have been advised of the rights I had.

Knowing your rights as a performer is part of your job as a performer. Many books focusing on the business of "show business" can be found in the Performing Arts section of most bookstores; take a look.

OUT CLAUSE

What if you get a better-paying and longer-term job while under contract with a theater? What are the ramifications if you leave your contracted job early?

When signing a contract it is very important to know what your "out clause" is. An out clause states how much notice you need to give the producer in order to legally terminate your contract. A contract can define this legal notice to be any length of time, though two or four weeks is standard.

You also must be sensitive to the producer's situation when giving the news that you intend to leave. What are the schedule, the budget, and the likelihood of replacing you? How far into production are you, and how essential is your role at this point? Is the theater located near a major city that has a pool of actors available to audition? While in theory the producer may wish you well, you may have caused a lot of grief right now. Some empathy on your part should make the conversation easier. The theater community is a small one, so you don't want to burn your bridges. On the other hand, if your producer does give you a hard time, you may not want to work for him or her again, anyway.

If the producer wants to terminate your contract, he or she, too, must comply with the agreed-upon out clause. If you are asked to leave immediately, then you must be given severance pay for the number of weeks defined as legal notice in the out clause. Most producers wouldn't fire you and then expect you to fulfill your contract for the remaining weeks of their out clause. It's fair to say that keeping a fired employee around would make for a very uncomfortable situation for everyone involved.

OUT OF TOWN: WHAT THE THEATER COMPANY PROVIDES AND REQUIRES

The following items may or may not apply to your first few jobs, but you might want to investigate all of them before taking any job out of town. Approach the management with inquiries—not with demands. You do not want to begin your relationship with a producer by having this person think of you as a needy, potentially problematic, demanding person with an attitude.

Transportation

Does the theater provide you with round-trip transportation from your home base to the job? Producers usually do, and should!

Housing

Is housing provided? Is the producer paying for it? Even though a producer housing you at his or her expense is commonplace, you should read the fine print in the contract.

Do not assume that all the luxuries of home will be waiting for you when you arrive at the cast's housing facilities. Be sure to read the contract carefully and make a list of any questions to ask before you leave your home. Usually the company manager contacts you to answer any questions you may have. If this doesn't happen and you are unsure of what to bring, call.

Don't take for granted the following:

- Alarm clock
- Bedding
- Kitchen facilities
- Your own room
- Coffee machine
- Fan
- Towels
- Laundry facility

Long-distance Telephone Service

Is there long-distance telephone service in the actor housing provided by the producer? Most theaters' cast-housing facilities do not provide any long-distance telephone service, the reason being that during your stay you might run up a large phone bill, then depart, leaving the producer stuck trying to find you to pay the bill. The cast housing will either provide a pay phone or a regular telephone with local service only. Therefore, you will need to have a calling card for long-distance calls or use your own cell phone.

Allergies

Most non-Equity actor housing does not have air-conditioning simply because the theater's management doesn't want to pay the electricity bill. If you suffer from severe allergies and need to have an air conditioner, this can be a huge problem. Find out about getting allergy shots and whether any local doctors in the area can treat your allergies if they worsen, or have your own doctor prescribe allergy medication for you before you leave town. Don't wait till you get to the job to realize that this could become a real problem.

Car

Is the housing close to the theater, grocery store, and gym? If the answer is "no," most theater companies, including those that are non-Equity, make several company cars available to the cast. Don't get too excited: these are usually old vehicles without air-conditioning, but they will get you where you need to go. Don't forget to bring your driver's license with you to the job.

If a theater does not provide cars, and the supermarket and laundry facilities are not within walking distance, then the management should organize some sort of system for transporting everyone weekly on an agreed-upon day (usually your day off).

Per Diem

"Per diem" means "per day." It's the amount of money paid to you weekly by the producer to cover such daily living expenses as food and lodging. Per diems are usually part of the contract only for touring shows. The money is untaxed and separate from your weekly salary. It is yours to use in whatever way you choose. If you pass through the city where your grandparents live, and you stay with them rather than in a hotel, the per diem is still yours to keep.

Here's another example: while on the national tour of the musical *Chicago*, as one of the conductors and pianists, I was given a per diem of approximately seven hundred dollars a week. When I arrived in Los Angeles for a five-month run, I found an old friend who happened to have an empty room in his house in West Hollywood. He offered to charge me six hundred dollars a month for rent. How could I say no? Consequently, during each of the five months that I lived there, I was able to save a lot of my per diem.

TECH WORK

Does your contract require you to do any tech work? Most non-Equity summer stock and dinner theaters require you to do jobs other than acting. Depending on your skills, you may be asked to help out in the costume shop by sewing and stitching, or in the scene shop by painting and building the set. Working behind the scenes is a great way to learn about what each of the departments contributes to a production, and how, together, they create the finished product. Be aware that this is not always mentioned in your contract, so don't be surprised when you are asked. (Better yet, ask before you sign the contract!)

Realize that few people—including professionals—make their living solely by acting. A summer stock situation can give you the equivalent of free lessons in related aspects of the business. These "lessons" could pay off in the long run by providing you with salable, complementary skills.

EQUITY MEMBERSHIP CANDIDATE (EMC)

As a non-union stage actor, you can earn "points" toward your Equity card through Actors' Equity Association's Equity Membership Candidate (EMC) Program. To register, you must first secure a qualifying position at an Equity theater that offers the program. Registration itself requires some paperwork and a fee ($100.00 in 2005) that will be credited toward your initiation fee when, ultimately, you are eligible to join the union. To earn your eligibility, you'll need to complete fifty "creditable weeks of work" at any theater authorized to offer the EMC program. One workweek equals one point. The fifty weeks do not have to be consecutive, and may be accumulated over any length of time. Equity's various agreements with theaters limit the types of work that can be credited, so when you're hired, you should check the company's rulebook for details. To get additional information about the EMC program, contact the nearest Equity office, or log onto the union Web site (www.actorsequity.org/Services/emc.html).

UNDERSTUDY OPPORTUNITIES

If you are debating whether to accept a show as a member of the chorus or ensemble, you might think about asking the director or producer whether you can be considered to understudy or eventually replace a principal performer. This could be the perk you are looking for, and performing the role might pay a little extra. If you have not handled a leading role in the professional theater before, then a great way to learn is by understudying.

If the theater company does agree to let you understudy a role, make sure that this job is written into your contract.

DECIDING TO STAY IN TOWN

Okay, you've been made an offer. You look over the contract, you network for reliable advice—and you decide to not accept. What will you do with your downtime? You must make a plan to stay active, and be careful to use your time and money wisely. Stay in class. Find new audition material. See as many shows as you can afford . . . and, of course, *keep auditioning.*

You can always find theater projects to get involved in—at least in lively theater cities like Boston, San Francisco, Minneapolis-St. Paul, Atlanta, Chicago, Los Angeles, and New York City. New York is rife with small performance spaces, and casting notices in *Back Stage* often seek actors and singers for readings or workshops of writers' new shows. If you can't find a performance opportunity looking for you, create your own by reading plays aloud with friends in the business.

Readings

"Readings" are presentations of new works in progress. As a performer in one of these projects, you are helping to develop a new show from its inception. If you are asked to participate in one, you should strongly consider taking the role. It's a great way to meet other actors and to witness the developmental process of a new play. The pay is usually very little, if any, but the experience can be invaluable.

A reading of a musical usually entails one week of rehearsals; plays generally rehearse for two or three days. Actors are not expected to memorize the script. For a staged reading, the actors are blocked with script in hand. For an unstaged reading, performers sit in chairs, or stand in one place.

A reading allows the authors and their invited guests to sit back and hear the unembellished script being read and/or sung by actors and singers. It helps the creators to gain perspective, to pinpoint the strengths and weaknesses in their work, and to figure out how to improve it.

Readings are often a way for actors to stay in the industry, maintain their skills, and network, while holding onto the nontheater jobs that pay their bills.

Do realize, though, that there are no guarantees you will be asked to stay with the piece if it should move on to a full production, or even just to another reading. Involvement in a reading is likely to be a one-shot deal.

Showcases

Another type of presentation is the "showcase," which is more enhanced than the reading. It is performed off book (meaning no script or music is in hand); adds staging, some costumes, scenery, lighting, and a scaled-down band (for a musical); and is usually better publicized.

Depending on the city you live in, this kind of low-budget production may or may not be covered by an Actors' Equity Association code or agreement. In New York, producers wanting to use Equity actors must file an application to produce under the Actors' Equity Association Showcase Code, which applies in theaters with ninety-nine seats or fewer. The Code covers everything from backstage conditions to advertising, from audition regulations to ticket prices. In lieu of salaries, it sets stipends or reimbursements, and it limits the number of performances. Showcases frequently rehearse at night and on weekends, so that performers can schedule around their "day jobs." New works, as well as revivals of old plays or musicals, are showcased.

Workshops

A workshop is more polished and more thoroughly staged than a reading or the usual showcase. If a show has been "picked up" by a producer, often a workshop will be presented as a final chance to hone or try out the production, and to get an audience's response. Most producers do not want to invest their money in a full production, fully in the public eye, until they feel the show is ready. Equity's Workshop Agreement, created for the development of new works, provides actors with salary and standard benefits. Under the agreement, performers who complete the workshop must be offered either the same role or function in the next production of the show under a standard Equity contract, or financial compensation if they are not hired back. One of the first shows that really defined the workshop was *A Chorus Line*.

Who Attends These Presentations?

Producers, investors, directors, casting directors, and agents are invited to see these presentations by the authors and artistic staff. Showcases are almost always advertised to the public, as well; readings and workshops may or may not be.

It is also your job to invite industry people to come see your work—that is, if you are being featured in a role that *truly shows off your talent and abilities*. You can turn off a casting director forever by inviting him or her to see a poorly mounted, under-rehearsed showcase in which you play a small and unchallenging part or give merely an adequate performance. It should be noted, too, that attracting casting people to even an excellent showcase is extremely difficult. Relatively few show up, simply because their workdays are very long, and they are inundated with dozens of invitations every week. In general, casting people are most likely to see a production that features many actors and is mounted by a producer that they recognize in an easily accessible (and safe) location.

Your producer (or his or her press agent) should keep a list of the industry people who actually have attended your show. You should then send each of these a thank-you note, probably with a headshot and résumé, in hopes that they will keep you on file for future projects.

Taking part in a reading, showcase, or workshop offers many perks in a short amount of time, without leaving town. Think about it: you have now met and worked with a director—and perhaps a musical director and choreographer—as well as actors you didn't know before. You have been seen by people in the industry—people who could cast you in the future. If you've read or showcased a new work, there is always the possibility that it will be produced and you will be asked to continue with it. How exciting to originate a role! Let the networking begin.

Demo Tapes

Many composers and lyricists promote their work by having their material recorded by actors. Singing on a demo tape gives you the opportunity to contribute artistically to a project from its inception. It also gives you a professionally produced tape, which comes in handy when a musical director needs to hear you on tape—because you are unable to attend an audition, for instance.

In addition to demo recordings, there are musical workshops for new writers—who, again, need singers to perform their material. Performers in workshops benefit from collaborating on a new project with its authors, and from being seen by those running and attending these sessions. The two most prominent workshops in New York City are sponsored by Broadcast Music Inc. (BMI) and the American Society of Composers, Authors, and Publishers (ASCAP).

Most of the time authors hire singers whom they have worked with before; however, their first choices might not always be available. Being recommended and word-of-mouth are usually the best way to get this kind of work, although solicitations do appear in the trades. Pay can be involved, depending on the producer and the nature of the project.

Readers

Casting directors constantly need readers. A "reader" is an actor who is hired to read the sides with the auditioning performers, so they have someone to play off of (to act with). As you become acquainted with casting directors, by all means write to them or tell them that you'd be interested in becoming a reader.

As a reader you have the advantage of being inside the audition room and seeing how other actors audition. You hear what the panel says about an actor after he or she has left the room. If you pay attention, you can learn a lot about how to improve your own audition performance.

In three different shows I was casting last year, the reader for each show was cast. All three performers were very talented, and happened to be the right types for the roles in question. Being hired as a reader isn't a common way to be cast in a show, but in each of these cases, the performer was (as the old saying goes) "in the right place at the right time." Once again, work leads to work!

Earning a Living

Waiting tables, catering, proofreading, market research, and temping (working for temporary employment agencies) are among the most common "job-jobs" that actors take to earn a living offstage. These occupations tend to offer the flexible hours that are critical for auditions and rehearsals. If you do not want to work in restaurants or the corporate world to pay your rent, look for flexible theater-related paying jobs. These can also offer perks—for instance, sales work at a theater bookstore gets you discounts on music, scripts, and books.

Many actors get to see Broadway and Off-Broadway shows for free by ushering or selling merchandise at the theater. You can also do telemarketing for a Broadway advertising agency, or for a performing arts network such as Lincoln Center. Most telemarketing supervisors insist that you see the show that you are selling—gee, what a chore. Working part-time in the box office of a theater is another great way to meet theater people and get free tickets.

Nontheater jobs like babysitting, pet sitting, dog walking, and tutoring offer the most flexibility in setting your own hours based around your audition schedule for the week. If you are creative and willing to do some research, you can find (or create) a lot of interesting and fun jobs.

Seeing Theater Inexpensively

There are many ways to see shows without spending a lot of money. In New York City, for instance, if you have a student ID you can get tickets for Broadway or Off-Broadway shows at a discounted price. Standing-room tickets are another way to see a show for less money. Most large Broadway theaters offer these, which literally assign you a spot in the back of the theater where you stand to watch the show. It's not the ideal way to view a performance, but it certainly beats paying for a full-price ticket that you can't afford.

Concert halls like Lincoln Center and Carnegie Hall always have student-priced seats, as well as "cheap" seats, costing as little as ten dollars. Check your local newspapers, trade publications, and Web sites for bargains and freebies. During the summer months, the weekly *Back Stage* lists most of the free concerts and plays that take place in Manhattan and other New York City boroughs.

Discount Tickets

Not-for-profit discount ticket booths can be found in many major theater cities. Among these are Hot Tix in Chicago, TKTS in New York City, TIX Bay Area in San Francisco, and Bostix in Boston. Ticketplace in Washington, D.C. offers online purchases as well. Available exclusively online are discount tickets in New Jersey (through njtheatrealliance.com) and Southern California (through LAStageAlliance.com). Services like these offer reduced-price tickets to shows—usually at fifty percent off. The drawback is that in most cases you can only purchase tickets on the day of the show—producers make discounted tickets available only when they know that they still have empty seats for the current performance.

In New York, for example, at about three o'clock in the afternoon, Broadway and Off-Broadway theaters that participate in the TKTS program look at their ticket sales for that evening's performance. (They start looking earlier on matinee days.) If they see a considerable number of available seats, they deliver those tickets to the TKTS booths in Times Square and at the South Street Seaport. The philosophy is that selling the remaining tickets at half price is better than not selling them at all. Obviously, a new hit show will not offer half-price tickets—especially on a Saturday night!

Another way of obtaining inexpensive tickets in your city is to look for an organization that buys blocks of discounted tickets for its members. New York has several of these; in return for paying an annual fee, their members receive offers throughout the year for tickets that have been considerably reduced in price.

Self-promotion: mailings

Sending out résumés and headshots to casting agencies is a great way to use your downtime. Mailings are necessary: it is your responsibility to make the industry aware of your availability. It is your job to send casting directors and agents your new headshot, your new phone number, new and noteworthy credits, an invitation to the show you are doing, etc.. It is your job to answer casting calls in the "trades," that is, to send photo-résumés or postcards to film and TV productions listed in the bimonthly *Ross Reports Television & Film* (see page 148) and posted for members on the Screen Actors Guild Web site.

It is *very* important that your mailings be purposeful and to the point. If you hear that a casting director is casting a show that you feel you are very right for, by all means, send your photo-résumé and a note. On the envelope, write "Attn: (Name of Show)," to give the casting director a reason to open it up and actually look at your materials. Most casting people don't have the time and/or staff to look at every unsolicited submission they receive in the mail.

If you decide to do a general mailing, *carefully* read about each casting office and agency to learn about its area of expertise. Some agencies handle actors only for theater; others handle only commercials or voice-overs; while still others focus only on theater, film, and television. Some seek only more-established actors or singers; others, only new or young talent; others, "all types." This information, as well as addresses, names, and titles of staff—and the ubiquitous "do not call or visit" warning—are published in *Ross Reports*. In New York and Los Angeles, preprinted mailing labels for agents and casting directors can be purchased at theater bookstores or through ads in the trades or on the Web.

Think before you mail your "stuff." Sending scattershot, unresearched mailings can be costly in two ways. First, constantly reproducing your headshots is expensive. Second, misdirected solicitations are a waste of casters' time, and a real turnoff—wouldn't you like potential employers to know that you can, indeed, read?

Classes

Staying in town gives you the opportunity to brush up on and stretch your skills. Acting classes, dance classes, voice lessons, coaching sessions, master classes, seminars, and lectures go on daily in large cities. (Their cost for you as a professional is tax deductible, and some are even free.)

If you simply cannot afford to take a class, then at least read books and scripts at your library. While you are there, listen to recordings of new and old shows that you are not familiar with, and borrow videos or DVDs. Approach your viewing as a student; this is not merely entertainment. Depending on your area of interest, pay attention to vocal production, acting style (or lack thereof), choreography, writing structure, orchestrations, direction, etc.

BUSINESS SMARTS

We know so many actors who are extraordinarily talented but have never reached any of their personal career goals. On the other hand, we know many not-so-talented actors who shouldn't be in the business but are hugely successful. Why? Is the business "unfair"? We don't think so. We think that you have to *decide* to succeed. You must believe in your talent. If succeeding is something that you really want, don't allow rejection to stop you.

STAYING ON COURSE

If like so many artists you favor wandering aimlessly, be prepared to accept the consequences. Many people like to taste and try a little bit of everything, especially when living in a large city like New York, Los Angeles, or Chicago. Nothing is wrong with that. However, if you choose not to stay on a focused path, you diminish your chances for success.

When I arrived in New York many years ago, I was ready to conquer the world. I wanted to be the most successful vocal coach, conductor, composer, arranger, and teacher. Once I saw how competitive the business was, I realized that to really excel in one area I would have to choose the dream job I wanted to achieve most and make all the others secondary (for a while at least).

Don't abandon all of your outside interests, but stay on track to reach what you want most right now.

DEFINING AND HAVING SUCCESS

Most importantly, you have to define what success means to you. For some it's about making money and becoming famous. For others, it is truly about being able to make a living as an actor and working on the stage with talented people.

Many actors say that working hard, continuing to study the craft, staying proactive, and maintaining a positive attitude are the key ingredients for obtaining success. By the same token, not being educated about, and/or not forcing yourself to be more aware of, the business of the "business" can often impede success.

Hundreds and hundreds of actors loaded with talent either don't understand or don't want to understand this "other" side of being a performer. Unfortunately, these actors give up too soon and leave the business. They believe their lack of success comes from lack of talent, but that is too often not the case. A successful store can't rely on ads it ran two years ago to bring in customers today.

After my first ten years of being in the business and paying my dues, I felt I had the right to sit back, relax, and let all of my hard effort work for me. That approach succeeded for about three years, and then the offers stopped. No one in the industry knew where I was. They all assumed I was out on the road with a show, or just busy working. But I was waiting for their calls. It never occurred to me that I had to keep informing directors and producers that I was *available* for work and interested in upcoming projects. I learned that if I wanted to continue having a career as a musical director in this competitive business, I could not let my pride get in the way of having to *constantly* promote myself.

CHAPTER 23

Representation

AGENTS

Two of the questions asked most often by young actors are "Do I need an agent?" and "If so, how do I get one?" First, let's define the function of an agent: this person submits your headshots and résumés to casting directors (see definition on pages 153–154), schedules your audition appointments, and relays to you exactly what the casting director is looking for. When you are offered a contract for a job, the details are given to your agent, who passes them on to you. If you and your agent are interested, you both need to decide whether anything missing in the contract is important to ask for: your own car, your own apartment, your own dressing room, special billing in the program and poster, etc. Similarly, you'll want to discuss whether anything stated in the contract should be changed—like your salary. Once you and your agent agree on your terms, your agent does all the negotiating for you, keeping in touch with you as it proceeds. Your agent may tell you that the producer is willing to offer one thing but can't deliver another.

At some point you and your agent decide whether to accept the offer, to keep pushing for the things you want, or simply to pass on the job.

Agent Commission

When an agency signs you, it is making an investment in your career. You never owe your agency money when you are not making money. Only when you book a job do both of you reap the financial benefits, in the same way a contingency lawyer gets paid only if you win a case. The standard commission for an agent is ten percent of your contract.

If an agency asks you for money simply for guiding your career, find a different agency quickly. This practice is dishonest in any state; in New York and California it is flat-out illegal. I can't reiterate enough that a reputable agency only makes money when you do!

Too Young?

Recently graduating from school should not discourage you from seeking an agent. Many agencies specialize solely in new and young talent. You can find them by studying *Ross Reports* and other trade publications.

If you are just starting out in the business, however, you may not *want* to have an agent. Non-Equity salaries are often low, and are usually not very negotiable. I don't know how you could afford to send your agent ten percent of a low salary. Once you move up to more high-profile jobs, become more established, and earn your Equity card, you will probably want to consider having an agent represent you.

Signing With an Agency

If an agent is somewhat interested in you, the agent may invite you to freelance with him or her for a while. This means that you are not contractually bound to this agent. If you find a job on your own, you do not have to report it to the agent, but if the agent submits you for an audition and you book the job, he or she must get ten percent. You can freelance with more than one agency at a time.

Once you do sign a contract committing to an agency, you are bound to it exclusively. Any job the agency gets for you, or you find on your own, must be reported to your agent. A standard minimum contract with an agency is for either two or three years.

Getting an Agent

There are many ways to attract an agent. The best begins with one seeing you perform live, onstage. Then it is your job to follow up with a letter and photo-résumé reminding the agent that he or she recently saw you in this show, and informing him or her that you are seeking representation. Remember that getting the agent to the show in the first place is also your job. Performing in readings, showcases, and workshops is a great way to be seen. Use the time before the show opens to send your flyer and cover letter to agents. Invite them to see your project—and, again, tell them that you are presently seeking representation.

Many performers have more than one agent. Sometimes, for instance, an actor has a great theater agent who doesn't deal in film and television, so the actor looks for a second agent who does. Modeling and voice-overs often require separate agents.

Ross Reports Television & Film

As noted earlier, information about talent agencies can be found in *Ross Reports Television & Film*. This bimonthly magazine covers casting information for New York, Los Angeles, San Diego, and San Francisco in each issue. *Ross Reports* gives contact and personnel information for agencies, casting directors, network television programs and production companies, and films in development and preparation. Throughout the year, special issues add sections focusing on areas ranging from cable TV production to animation and voice-over work. Additionally, *Ross Reports* publishes four annual directories: the *USA Talent Directory*, listing agents and casting directors throughout the United States; the *Film Casting and Production Directory*; the *Television Commercial Casting and Production Directory*; and *Ross Reports Guide to Modeling for Commercial, Print, Television & Film*.

The magazine is published bimonthly because of high turnover and rapid changes in the industry: new casting and agency offices open, veterans close or splinter off, personnel and addresses change, and TV and film production companies come and go. *Ross Reports* is available at theater bookstores and most branches of Borders and Barnes & Noble. You can also subscribe online at www.rossreports.com. The Web site is updated monthly.

Writing a Letter

Unfortunately, you won't always be in a position to invite agents to see you onstage. When you're not performing, I encourage you to write to agencies letting them know you are seeking representation.

Step One Begin by sending a brief cover letter with your headshot and résumé. Your letter should simply state that you are new to the business, yet eager to get started in the professional world. You've heard great things about the agency and would like very much to be considered for an interview and/or audition. Most agents respond favorably to referrals, so if an actor friend is already represented by the agency, ask for permission to use his or her name in your letter. Most agencies see new people a couple of times a year, to update their files.

Step Two Follow up one to three weeks later with a photo postcard. Or, if you are fortunate enough to be performing onstage at this point, send the agency an invitation with a reminder letter or postcard stating that you have written before and are following up.

An example of what an agent-seeking letter might look like appears on page 150. It shows all you need to include in your letter. The agent knows what you want. If you write a longer letter delving into your past, where you are from, and where you see yourself in ten years, he or she won't read most of it. Be patient. Keep working and keep persevering. When the time is right you will find an agent.

Ask Friends

Another method used frequently to meet an agent is to ask your friends with agents how their agencies go about seeing potential clients. As noted, often a letter with your friend's referral can get you in the door. (Again, make sure you ask your friends first.)

You Are Still in Charge

Be careful not to sign with the first agency that wants you. Ask other actors what they know about the firm. Look for an agent who is young and enthusiastic like yourself. Find someone hungry to make money and to become established as a successful representative. The more excited the agent is about you, the more auditions you will be sent on.

If your agency gets too easygoing about sending you out, it is your job to keep pushing it to promote you. If that doesn't work, you should probably start searching for another agent.

Your Name
Address
Phone Number

Date

Agent's Name
Agency Name
Address

Dear _____:

I am a recent graduate of _____ (insert your school),
and am presently seeking representation. I have read and researched a lot
about _____ (insert agency name), and feel I can be
a great addition to your clientele. I am very driven and eager to start my
journey in the "business."

    Enclosed are my headshot and résumé. Thank you for your time and
consideration. I look forward to hearing from you soon.

Sincerely,

Sample agent-seeking letter

With or without an agent, you are always your own business manager and promoter. Only you are responsible for your own career. While others can guide you, you must lead the way. It is *your* job to make the industry aware of your existence and your desire to work.

Having an agent doesn't mean that you can sit back and wait for the work to come to you. Even the best agents can get lazy or overworked. Even a small agency has many clients, and can't spend all of its time managing and focusing on your career. You need to inform your agent of projects that you are interested in—projects that the agent might have overlooked or hadn't thought of submitting you for.

Note: There is a big difference between being a good businessperson who is assertive and an actor who is annoyingly aggressive. An assertive businessperson self-promotes by staying visible to the industry through auditions and performances. He or she follows up on something started, knowing no one else will do it. An annoying actor doesn't know when he or she is bothering people, or when to stop. This person shows up at his or her agent's office unannounced or calls the agency daily without a specific question. You must find for yourself the fine line that separates the two.

I am often surprised at the number of actors who repeat "If I can just get an agent, if I can just get an agent . . ." My usual response is, "Yes—and then what?" What happens after you get that agent? Your career doesn't suddenly change because you have representation. Having an agent makes you more accessible to casting directors because the performers they first call in to audition are usually agents' submissions.

We have found this difference between actors who have agents and actors who don't: actors without agents are hungry to work, constantly going to any audition they can find, getting up at five in the morning to wait in line to *possibly* be seen at an audition. Actors with agents generally wait for their agents to call them. If you ask most actors with agents whether they are content with how much work they get, they will tell you, "No." If you also ask them whether their agents are doing enough to further their careers, they will usually tell you, "No." In defense of agents, however, many actors aren't able to see and admit that they themselves aren't working very hard to help their own careers.

BREAKDOWN SERVICES

Breakdown Services is a paid service subscribed to by agents and managers, but unavailable to the public. When a casting director is ready to schedule appointments for an audition, he or she fills out a "breakdown." This list of all the roles being cast includes each character's name and approximate age, a brief description, required vocal range, etc. The breakdown also states the name of the theater/production company, the artistic team, rehearsal and performance dates, and some-

I'm gonna make ya famous, kid!...
You'll be perfect for the Dancing Monkey! Just perfect!

times the salaries being offered. The casting director sends the completed break-down to Breakdown Services for distribution to its subscribers.

On any given morning, an agent or manager can find thirty different break-downs from many different casting directors. It is each agent's job to read these breakdowns carefully and decide which clients should be submitted to a casting director for an audition.

MANAGERS

A manager is like an agent in that he or she may subscribe to Breakdown Services and can submit actor clients for auditions, but differs from an agent by not being licensed to negotiate contracts and similar financial matters. This person's job, according to the National Conference of Personal Managers, is to provide "advice and counsel."

More than an agent, a manager nurtures your career by helping guide you to areas of study and assisting you in making career decisions. This close professional relationship is particularly useful in the developmental stages of your career. An agent assumes that you know your craft already and doesn't usually take—or have—the time to help you find places to study.

Generally, agents are regulated by state business law, but managers are not. The performers unions grant franchises to qualified agents, but there are no such franchises for managers. Commission rates differ, as well: in New York and California, for example, an agent cannot legally collect a commission of more than ten percent on any job booked for a client. Although most reputable managers collect no more than fifteen percent, this ceiling is not determined by law. You should, of course, research any representative before contracting with him or her. This is especially true of managers because they are not legally regulated.

You will also hear the term "manager" used in reference to celebrities' assistants. The duties of this type of manager can include traveling with a client on the road, and making sure that every term in the client's rider has been met. Such managers also deal with each theater or concert hall's management, so that the performers they are representing don't have to.

CASTING DIRECTORS

To cast its upcoming show, a theater or producer generally employs a casting director. The casting director is informed in detail as to what the theater/director is looking for, such as the size of the cast, character descriptions, vocal needs (for a musical), and base salaries. Using this information, the casting director sends out a cast breakdown to numerous theatrical agencies. Each agency submits appropriate clients to the casting director. The casting director, in turn, decides exactly whom to schedule for an appointment.

A casting director can receive hundreds or even thousands of submissions for any given project. Usually, he or she will look at agents successfully dealt with in the past, as well as actors called in before and admired. Remember that your agent's submission does not guarantee that the casting director will call you in to audition. Many coaches will tell you that casting directors are more important to know than agents, or even producers, since casting directors choose which actors will be seen.

The producer gives the casting director a budget within which to cast the show. The casting director figures out how many days of auditions the budget will cover—including expenses such as renting an audition space and hiring a pianist. It then becomes the casting director's responsibility to schedule the number of actors who can be seen in the allotted time—usually in ten-minute slots.

Do you need to have an agent in order to be called in by a casting director? No, but having one makes it more likely. The casting director seeks actors who are very good matches for each project. Where they are found really doesn't matter. Part of the casting director's job is to attend readings, showcases, workshops, or university showcases in search of new talent.

Being Submitted

When you are called in by a casting director, *always* be on time for your scheduled audition. ("On time" should be five or ten minutes early.) You must be fully prepared to perform the material that you have been asked to bring in. Your agent will send or have you pick up "sides" (see "'Sides' and 'Cold Readings,'" page 51, in Chapter 7) that the director wants you to read, or the breakdown will be specific about the type of song or monologue the panel wants to hear at the audition. If you embarrass the casting director in front of the producer by showing up ill prepared, the producer may not hire the casting director for the next show. It can take a long time for that casting director to forgive and forget—he or she may never call you again. If, however, you *are* on time and well prepared, all you need to concern yourself with is auditioning well.

Auditioning to Take Over a Role

If you are being considered to replace, understudy, or stand by for a particular actor, see the production before your audition. Approach the character in the way you see it performed by the current actor, at least in terms of general style and tone. If the actor originated the role or was the first replacement, then this person was directed by either the production's director or assistant director—so what he or she is doing is probably what the creative team wanted. (Normally, any further replacements are put into the show by the stage manager, especially if the production is touring. The responsibilities of the assistant director and the stage manager include maintaining the integrity of the director's work by calling brushup, understudy, and replacement rehearsals.)

Keep in mind that your function as a replacement is not to reinvent a role. If it ain't broke, don't fix it. The fact that *you* are now doing the role automatically makes it different. Of course, you will be speaking the same lines and taking the same blocking and direction as your predecessor, but simply because you are your own person with your own history and background, your performance will be unique.

Celebrity replacements are an exception to the rule of not reinventing a role. For instance, when Glenn Close, who created the role of Norma Desmond in Broadway's *Sunset Boulevard*, was leaving, the producers asked Betty Buckley to take over. The director did not hire or expect Miss Buckley to perform the role in same way that Miss Close had. He knew that Miss Buckley, a seasoned performer with a distinctive style, would serve and shape the role in her own way.

Julie Andrews created the lead in Broadway's *Victor/Victoria*. She was eventually replaced by Liza Minelli and Raquel Welch. Each of these actresses was obviously hired for her unique persona (and box office draw). Clearly they have few similarities, yet they all successfully performed the same role, probably never having seen each other's performance.

More Mailings

As with agents, you should send casting directors your picture and résumé when you are performing in something that they can see you in—again, use *Ross Reports* and other trade publications to research your mailing.

Don't forget that directors, musical directors, and choreographers keep résumés and headshots of actors who have auditioned well for them in the past. You may get a random call from a casting director to audition for a director whom you don't even know. That's most likely because you auditioned for that director before, and/or this person saw your work onstage.

A few summers ago I received a call from a producer offering me work at his theater. I was curious about how he got my name and number, so he told me that he'd had my résumé on file since I had sent it—five years before. Mailings do pay off . . . maybe just not right away.

CHAPTER 24

Actors' Equity Association

Actors' Equity Association (AEA) is the major union for professional theater actors in the United States. The American Guild of Musical Artists (AGMA) and the American Guild of Variety Artists (AGVA) also represent stage performers. The Screen Actors Guild (SAG) and the American Federation of Television and Radio Artists (AFTRA) have jurisdiction over film, television, and commercials. Each of these unions has different rules and procedures for governing and protecting their membership. Since this book is meant for stage actors, this chapter will focus on Equity.

You become a member of AEA either when a theater hires you under an Equity contract, or when you complete the Equity Membership Candidate (EMC) Program. (See Chapter 22, "Getting Experience," page 134.) Either way, you'll pay a one-time initiation fee, plus semi-annual membership dues. In 2005 the initiation fee was $1,100, and basic dues were $118.00 yearly.

Joining Equity—or any union, for that matter—should not be a frivolous or temporary decision. Ultimately, it is a lifelong affiliation and obligation. The union only survives because its members have made this informed commitment.

HOW LONG SHOULD YOU STAY NON-UNION (NON-EQUITY)?

Deciding whether to take your Equity card or to remain non-union is an individual decision. It depends on whether you have committed yourself to acting as a career, and whether you and others in the business believe that your talent and work ethic have matured enough to compete with dedicated professionals. Remember, once you become a member of AEA, you can no longer audition for non-Equity jobs; and if you choose to withdraw from the union, rejoining it will be much more difficult.

It is wise to build a foundation of experience for a few years in non-Equity theaters and performance venues. They will give you a chance to handle large roles, learn theater terminology and professional etiquette, and build up self-confidence. If you become a member of Equity without a lot of practical experience, you are still expected to know how to work and behave professionally.

Many Equity agreements give union companies an AEA–non-union ratio: the producers are allowed to hire a specified percentage of non-union actors each season. This saves the theaters money, because even when they pay union and non-union actors the same salaries, they aren't obliged to provide the non-union people with health insurance, to reimburse them for travel expenses, or to underwrite their housing.

Still, working as a non-union actor in one of these companies can be a great way to get experience, and to see what union membership gives and how union members behave. Theaters are most likely to fill their non-union quota with younger, less-experienced actors. This is because parts for younger people (especially in classics) usually are less demanding emotionally and artistically than are roles for more mature actors. A wise producer would not want to pay Equity wages plus benefits to a novice actor in a relatively undemanding role. That producer would more logically and usefully allocate his AEA quota for veteran actors who can play the more difficult roles.

Although Equity has procedures for going on hiatus and for leaving the union altogether, these are not frivolous decisions. You cannot leapfrog in and out of Equity job-by-job or on a whim.

WHAT YOU GET WHEN YOU JOIN

Benefits of becoming Equity include:

- Regulated salary protection

- Set rehearsal hours after which overtime pay applies

- Rehearsal breaks every sixty or ninety minutes

- Out-of-town housing standards

- Round-trip transportation to and from out-of-town theaters

- Required days off

- Health insurance contribution

- Retirement pension plan contribution

- Clothing rental if your own clothing is used onstage

- Moving-scenery regulations—certain Equity contracts do not allow actors to move furniture on and off stage, unless they are compensated.

AEA has more than thirty agreements and codes. They vary because they govern productions in many kinds of venues and formats (e.g., "Business Theatre and Events" "Cabaret," "Dinner Theatre"), under wide-ranging budgets, and with different seating capacities. Some are specific to certain cities or regions. Some of the national agreements are:

- Council of Resident Stock Theatres (CORST)

- Council of Stock Theatres (COST)

- Guest Artist

- Letter of Agreement (LOA)

- League of Resident Theaters (LORT)

- Musical Stock/Unit Attraction (MSUA)

- Outdoor Drama

- Production (Broadway/National Tours)

- Small Professional Theatre (SPT)

- Theatre for Young Audiences (TYA)

- University/Resident Theatre Association (URTA)

A complete listing with detailed information about AEA can be found on its Web site: www.actorsequity.org.

"CRASHING" AN EQUITY AUDITION

Most theaters operating under Equity agreements are required by the union to hold one or more days of annual "open" auditions for AEA members. These enable union actors without agents or managers to be seen by someone with casting authority. Non-union actors may go to these auditions; most theaters will see them at the end of the audition day, if there is time. This approach requires tenacity and patience, but people do get seen and even cast this way. At the very least, you may be put in the casting director's or director's file for a later project: networking!

OTHER THEATRICAL UNIONS

Theater, of course, is the collaborative effort of many different professions. Most of these nonactors have their own unions. For instance:

American Federation of Musicians (AF of M)

Association of Theatrical Press Agents and Managers (ATPAM)

The Dramatists Guild of America (DGA)

International Alliance of Theatrical Stage Employees (IATSE)

National Association of Talent Representatives (NATR)

Screen Actors Guild (SAG)

Society of Stage Directors & Choreographers (SSDC)

United Scenic Artists (USA)

SETTING YOUR STANDARDS

Once you have started to get the hang of auditioning, and begin to get work, you should consider setting standards and goals for your career. How you perceive yourself is how the industry will see you.

A lot of actors don't consider themselves to be leading men or women. They acknowledge that their strengths are in singing, dancing, and playing bit parts in the ensemble. These performers can often go from show to show, always working in the chorus. By their own definition they are successfully doing what they want to be doing.

On the other hand, there are actors and singers who aspire to play principal roles, whether romantic or character leads. These performers know that when first starting out they will have to pay their dues by taking small roles and jobs in the chorus, to gain experience and to be in a learning environment. If you are one of these performers, there will come a time when you must decide whether you are ready to move out of the chorus and tackle a principal role. This might entail turning down chorus work for a while. Getting jobs in the theater on any level does not come easy; competition is stiff. Therefore, you will constantly have to decide whether not working for six months to a year is worth the wait for a role.

For example, when I first moved to New York City, I knew that the path to becoming a musical director and conductor was to take jobs as a pianist in the orchestra pit. Two years later, I was being offered more pianist work than I could handle. That's when I realized it was time to leave the pit, and to start convincing directors and producers that I could conduct. Though it was difficult at times to turn down very credible and well-paying jobs as a pianist, I knew I was ready to move on. Within a year, I started to get shows as an assistant conductor, and applied for work out of town to gain experience as a musical director. When I returned with experience and my new and updated résumé, I was finally seen as a musical director.

CHAPTER 25

Resources

Trade publications and Web sites, libraries and bookstores, and membership organizations and networking events: all of these valuable resources are available to actors in most cities. With the Internet, of course, your networking prospects are "virtually" unlimited—but so are con artists' opportunities to rip you off. Imagination, energy, and skill will lead you to work—but don't lose your common sense along the way. In the twenty-first century, you still don't get something for nothing: anything that looks too easy probably is; and a classy ad campaign can promote a time-wasting, career-stalling, money-guzzling scam.

A variety of established, reputable service organizations and publications can point you toward potential employment, and help with your research—wherever you live in the United States. A few samples follow.

DIRECTORIES ONLINE AND IN PRINT

Two annual directories that are particularly useful for young actors are American Theatre Works' *Summer Theatre Directory* and *Regional Theatre Directory*. The first lists about 350 summer theaters, theme parks, and summer training programs; the second profiles more than 400 regional theaters in the United States. Both books are aimed at job-hunting performers, designers, technicians, and administrators, so they offer details not often found on individual theaters' Web sites: from where and when auditions are held and résumés may be submitted, to housing and transportation policies, to length of season and number of actors/apprentices hired. Information is available at www.theatredirectories.com.

Another resource is Theatre Communications Group's (TCG's) annual *Theatre Directory*. TCG, which describes itself as "the national organization for the American not-for-profit theatre," offers a number of services, a great deal of information, and many publications to its 400-plus member theaters and thousands of individual members. The directory lists member theaters' contact information, annual budgets, contracts, and special interests. Far more detailed descriptions of the theaters can be found on TCG's Web site, in *Theatre Profiles*. Information can be found at www.tcg.org.

Two other service organizations for theaters that carry lists and links for members are The Institute of Outdoor Drama (IOD) and the Shakespeare Theatre Association of America (STAA). The IOD represents about forty-five historical dramas, sixty-five Shakespeare Festivals, and eleven religious dramas throughout the United States. Its publications include the annual *Directory of Outdoor Drama in America.* Information is available at www.unc.edu/depts/outdoor. The STAA's 80-plus full members represent indoor, outdoor, year-round, seasonal, and university-affiliated Shakespeare companies, both Equity and non-union. For information, go to www.staaonline.org.

NEW YORK, NEW YORK

Hundreds of actors head for New York City every year. It certainly is not the only lively, thriving theater town in the country—but it *is* the biggest community of stage performers in the United States. In 2004, when Actors' Equity Association had 39,544 active members, 15,654 lived in the New York area. Los Angeles came next, with 7,557, then Chicago, with 1,355. Equity's top ten also included San Francisco, Washington, D.C./Baltimore, Boston, Orlando, Minneapolis/St. Paul, and Seattle (each with fewer than 1,000 members).

Those who plan to call the Big Apple home can find themselves overwhelmed by "resources" when they arrive. Here are just a few places where researching and networking can start.

Back Stage

Back Stage has been mentioned earlier in this book. Sub-headlined "The Actor's Resource," it's a weekly trade paper that lists upcoming auditions for theater, film, television, cabaret, student projects, workshops of new projects, cruise ships, theme parks, and more. These casting notices are submitted to the paper by the producer or casting people for each production, or are picked up from Actors' Equity. The productions listed are being mounted by theater companies all over the country, which send their representatives to New York auditions. The notices include the name of the production company and the show(s) being cast, performance (and sometimes rehearsal) dates, the place and time of the audition, character breakdowns, and whether or not the show is under a union contract. Usually the notices at least indicate the style of the show or film so that actors can choose appropriate audition material.

Back Stage also carries classified and display advertisements for performance-related products and services, as well as breaking news and updates about the business of theater in New York and around the country. Its editorial section includes features that keep newcomers in mind—from how to find the "right" photographer, class, or agent, to what to expect when you're hired by a theme park or a cruise line. One weekly column focuses on regional theater in more than a dozen cities; others cover topics ranging from book reviews to legal matters specific to performers. The paper also reviews shows Off-, Off-Off-, and on Broadway; dance; and cabaret.

Back Stage is available at newsstands in New York City and some of its suburbs, and by subscription. It is by no means the only stage actors newspaper in the country.

In Los Angeles, for instance, *Back Stage West* carries casting notices, features, columns, news, and advertisements for the greater Los Angeles area. In Chicago, *PerformInk* does the same for Chicago- and Milwaukee-based actors. Available in print bi-monthly—and online at www.performink.com—*PerformInk* defines itself as "Chicago's Entertainment Trade Paper," covering "the art, the business, the industry." National publications include the venerable *Variety* and the film-oriented *Hollywood Reporter*.

Both *Back Stage* and *Back Stage West* are online at www.backstage.com. This Web site also provides editorial and casting information for other major theater/stage locales, such as Chicago, Las Vegas, and Florida.

What's Missing

Many auditions are not published in casting notices. If the producer/casting people have chosen not to see the general population of actors, and if their production is not covered by an Actors' Equity agreement requiring them to hold "open" auditions for union members, you won't find their casting notice in the trades. Actors with agents or managers have the advantage here, because their representatives can subscribe to Breakdown Services. Actors who lack representation, but are focused, self-confident, and diplomatic networkers, can find some of these auditions on their own.

Scams

Reputable trade publications do their best to identify bogus casting notices and advertisements, and refuse to run them. But you need to look out for yourself, too. Be *extremely* wary of auditions or callbacks in private apartments. Don't believe in ads that promise "big money or featured roles—no experience required." Many nontrade papers run such classifieds, which are lures to hook actors and models into paying hundreds of dollars for photos, placement in headshot books, or listings in directories. The photos are pathetic, the headshot books are never printed, and the directories go to producers who don't want them.

Do your research on people and theaters that you haven't heard of before sending them your picture and résumé. Look for a Web site, and ask other actors what they know about the company; contact your local Equity office for information about union theater companies. As was stressed in Chapter 20, do *not* put your home address and telephone number—or social security number!—on your résumé.

On the Web . . .

Several Web sites highlighting New York City theater carry information about regional companies and productions, as well. Among these are:

- www.playbill.com (includes lists for New York and regional/touring theater, casting/job listings, news and features, ticket sales, buzz, archives)

- http://www.theatermania.com (includes listings for New York and "spotlight" cities, news and columns, reviews of New York and regional productions, ticket sales, archives)
- talkinbroadway.com (includes New York and regional theater news, reviews, and interviews, Broadway history, chat, archives)

The Internet Broadway Database (www.ibdb.com) archives New York theater productions from the nineteenth century until today, in detail.

. . . and on Foot

Research can still be done the old-fashioned way—away from your computer. In major theater cities you'll find stores that specialize in theater books and music or that feature Performing Arts departments, or libraries with theater and music sections. For example, New York City's numerous resources include these specialists in sheet music, scripts, and recordings:

The Colony (a large selection of old standards, scores, composer anthologies, pop and rock music, recordings, and vocal selections)
(212) 265-2050
1619 Broadway (Broadway and 49th Street)

The Drama Bookstore (a large selection of scores, vocal selections, and scripts)
(212) 944-0595
250 West 40th Street

New York Public Library for the Performing Arts (one of the largest lending performing arts libraries in the country, with recordings, books, scores, original documents, and a listening and viewing center)
(212) 870-1630
40 Lincoln Center Plaza (Broadway and 65th Street)

CHAPTER 26

Actors' Taxes

An actor's taxes can be complicated. If you're lucky, you'll have several jobs in a single year. This means that the following January, you'll receive W-2 forms from several employers, detailing your salary and deductions. Additionally, your jobs may be out of town, so at the end of the year, you'll need to report to more than one state, as well as to the Internal Revenue Service (IRS). If you're like most actors, you'll probably have one or more "job-jobs," for which you'll also receive W-2—or 1099—forms.

Rather than taking people on as salaried employees (W-2), some theaters prefer to hire workers on a fee basis (1099). If you are contracted to be paid a fee of $500 per week, your weekly check will be for the entire $500. The theater will not have withheld taxes, Social Security, F.I.C.A., etc., and you will receive a 1099 form in January or February instead of a W-2 form. It is up to you to remember that *you* are responsible for paying these monies that were not withheld! The good news is that as an actor you'll also have many job and job-hunting expenses that can be deducted from your gross income. These deductions can help reduce your taxes.

When an employer hires you for a salaried position, you will be asked to fill out a W-4 form; if you're working as an independent contractor, you'll be given a W-9. The W-4 will ask you how many dependents you want to claim; the W-9 will not.

If you are single and expect to work several freelance jobs during the year, you should seriously consider claiming *zero* dependents on your W-4 form. This way the highest-allowed amount of tax will be taken from your paycheck, and you won't have to pay tax on this job when you file for the year. If you claim *one* dependent (you are your own dependent), you'll put a little money back in your weekly check, but you will most likely owe the difference at tax time.

Now, the government acknowledges that it takes money to make money, so it allows you to deduct (write off) certain allowable business expenses. However, first you must prove on your tax returns that you are an entertainer, performer, or actor. If you haven't earned any money yet as a performer, you cannot write off any expenses related to the "business." That would be like someone trying to write off every meal you ate because you were thinking of becoming a chef.

Be sure to save all of your receipts for expenses related to the "business." Sometimes I purposely buy an item that I know can be used as a legitimate deduction, to reduce my taxes. For instance, several years ago I knew that I would owe a lot of money, so rather than writing a check for $2,000 to the government, I bought a new computer and other items that were deductible. Yes, I still spent the money, but at least I had something to show for it.

Tax laws regarding deductions change from year to year. This is one of many good reasons to have a knowledgeable accountant who handles taxes for performers. Your accountant will know which deductions are allowable each year.

All of this means that you'll need to be a conscientious, methodical record keeper. It is *absolutely* important that you keep a careful record of all your earnings, backed up with pay stubs, and a careful record of all your expenditures, backed up with receipts. You'll need this information when tax time rolls around. You'll be grateful that you kept well-ordered receipts when you sit down with your accountant and start weighing income against deductions. A methodical record keeper is probably not what you went into the business to become. But, again, acting is a business—and you are your own chief executive officer and bookkeeper.

SOME DEDUCTIONS FOR PERFORMERS
(Not all of these apply to everyone)

Last year's paid taxes	(Federal)	$_____
	(State)	$_____
	(City)	$_____
Tax preparation fees		$_____
Prescription drugs not paid by insurance		$_____
Medical and dental not paid by insurance		$_____
Interest on student loans		$_____
Union yearly membership dues		$_____
Computer expenses		$_____
CDs, tapes, books		$_____
Photocopying music and scripts		$_____
Music/dance carrying bag		$_____
Walkman (for rehearsals)		$_____
Sheet music		$_____

Theater tickets $_____

Subscriptions to entertainment magazines $_____

Cable TV (partial deduction) $_____

Video rentals (industry related) $_____

Telephone business expenses $_____

Answering service/voice mail $_____

Business meals (to discuss your own career) $_____

Business transportation $_____

Opening-night gifts $_____

Stage makeup $_____

Voice lessons/coaching $_____

Dance class $_____

Dance clothes $_____

Rehearsal space rental $_____

Headshots/reproductions $_____

Résumés $_____

Postage $_____

Faxing $_____

Mailing labels $_____

Office supplies $_____

Hotels $_____

Business-related rental cars $_____

CHAPTER 27

In Conclusion

If you can think these thoughts before each audition, you will alleviate much of your stress; you will have a clearer, more positive attitude before you enter the audition room and after you leave it:

> *"This is who I am today. This is my hair color, my weight, my height, my voice range, my age range, and these are my acting abilities today. If you can use me, that would be great; if not, thank you for letting me audition for you today—for the opportunity to audition one more time. I know the reason you may not be interested in me has nothing do to with anything I did incorrectly, because I was very well prepared."*

Here's a metaphor to help put you in the mind of a casting person: imagine shopping in an immense furniture store for a new couch, and narrowing your choices down to three couches that fit into your price range and color scheme, and reflect your preferences in size and shape. Which factors will help you decide which one of those three to take home? Any of them would be just fine in your living room. Ultimately, your own gut feeling and personal taste will dictate your decision. The process of casting from an audition works in much the same way. Often you will give a great audition and know that you are very right for the show, yet you won't get called back because you don't embody the vision or personal taste of the director. You can do nothing to change that. You must learn to accept the reality that casting a show is a very subjective process. If you don't, you'll drive yourself crazy with second-guessing, self-recrimination, and overanalysis.

Yet—unlike the inanimate couch in my metaphor—you *do* have the power to *not* be powerless. Start seeing yourself as a well-educated artist entering the business of your choice. And remember that word: *business*. Your agent will collect a ten percent commission from you; what will you do to earn the other ninety percent? Sure, you are the one working onstage or in front of the camera, but what do you do *offstage* or *off* camera? It is your job to stay on top of your career by studying the trade publications, taking classes, networking, and keeping your eyes and ears constantly open for information.

Don't be too hard on yourself in your chosen profession. Remember why you entered it in the first place. Work hard, set standards—but also find time to laugh, take a walk, turn off your brain, sit up all night with friends, and, please, have conversations about something other than the theater!

Have *fun*. Enjoy your journey.

Break a leg!

Audition Song List

The song lists below are simply suggestions of usable audition material for musical theater auditions. There are thousands and thousands of songs that are not listed, so view these lists as a starting place in your ongoing search for appropriate material.

I listed the show or film that each song originated from (or ended up in). You will find many of the shows were never published; however, if you refer to the composer and lyricist (also noted) you can find those songs in their respective anthologies. For example, "You'd Be Surprised," written by Irving Berlin, is from a show called *Ziegfeld Follies of 1919*. It is safe to assume that you will not find the score to that show; however, you will find the song in the *Irving Berlin Anthology*.

MALE UPTEMPO

Song	Show/Film	Composer & Lyricist
"After Today"	Doctor Doolittle (Film)	Leslie Bricusse & Anthony Newley
"Alas For You"	Godspell	Stephen Schwartz
"All I Care About"	Chicago	John Kander & Fred Ebb
"All I Need is the Girl"	Gypsy	Jule Styne & Stephen Sondheim
"Big News"	Parade	Jason Robert Brown
"Big Bow Wow, The"	Snoopy	Larry Grossman and Hal Hackady
"Big Black Man"	The Full Monty	David Yazbek
"Big News"	Parade	Jason Robert Brown
"Bigger Isn't Better"	Barnum	Cy Coleman & Michael Stewart
"Broadway Baby"	Dames At Sea	Jim Wise & George Haimsohn
"Buddy's Blues"	Follies	Stephen Sondheim
"Come With Me"	The Boys From Syracuse	Richard Rodgers & Lorenz Hart
"Cover Girl"	Cover Girl (Film)	Jerome Kern & Ira Gershwin
"Dear Old Syracuse"	The Boys From Syracuse	Richard Rodgers & Lorenz Hart
"Don Jose of Far Rockaway"	Wish You Were Here	Harold Rome
"Don't Get Around Much Anymore"	Sophisticated Ladies	Duke Ellington & Bob Russell
"Don't Marry Me"	Flower Drum Song	Richard Rodgers & Oscar Hammerstein
"Ev'rybody Has The Right To Be Wrong"	Skyscraper	James Van Heusen & Sammy Cahn
"Ev'rything I've Got"	By Jupiter	Richard Rodgers & Lorenz Hart
"Everybody Says Don't"	Anyone Can Whistle	Stephen Sondheim
"Extraordinary"	Pippin	Stephen Schwartz
"Fabulous Feet"	The Tap Dance Kid	Henry Krieger & Robert Lorick
"Fidgety Feet"	Oh, Kay!	George & Ira Gershwin
"Floozies"	The Grass Harp	Claibe Richardson & Kenward Elmsie
"Forty-Five Minutes From Broadway"	George M!	George M. Cohan
"From This Moment On"	Out of This World	Cole Porter
"Giants in the Sky"	Into The Woods	Stephen Sondheim
"Girls"	Mexican Hayride	Cole Porter
"Golden Rainbow"	Golden Rainbow	Walter Marks
"Good Times Are Here To Stay"	Dames at Sea	Jim Wise & George Haimsohn
"Gotta Dance"	Look Ma, I'm Dancin'	Hugh Martin
"Grand Knowing You"	She Loves Me	Jerry Bock & Sheldon Harnick
"Half As Big As Life"	Promises, Promises	Burt Bacharach & Hal David
"Happy As The Day is Long"	Cotton Club Parade (22nd edition)	Harold Arlen & Ted Koehler

Song	Show	Composer & Lyricist
"Heaven on Their Minds"	*Jesus Christ Superstar*	Andrew Lloyd Webber & Tim Rice
"Herod's Song"	*Jesus Christ Superstar*	Andrew Lloyd Webber & Tim Rice
"Hey There, Good Times"	*I Love My Wife*	Cy Coleman & Michael Stewart
"How Could You Believe Me When I Said …"	*Royal Wedding* (Film)	Irving Berlin
"How To Succeed"	*How To Succeed in Business Without Really Trying*	Frank Loesser
"I Can't Be Bothered Now"	*My One and Only* and *Crazy For You*	George & Ira Gershwin
"I Can't Give You Anything But Love"	*Blackbirds of 1928*	Jimmy McHugh & Dorothy Fields
"I Can't Stand Still"	*Footloose*	Dean Pitchford & Tom Snow
"I Feel a Song Comin' On"	*Every Night at Eight*	Jimmy McHugh & Dorothy Field
"I, Huckleberry Me"	*Big River*	Roger Miller
"I Found a New Baby"	*Thoroughly Modern Millie*	Jack Palmer & Spencer Williams
"I Got Plenty of Nuttin'"	*Porgy and Bess*	George Gershwin & Duboise Heyward
"I Like Everybody"	*The Most Happy Fella*	Frank Loesser
"I Love a Film Cliché'"	*A Day in Hollywood— A Night in the Ukraine*	Frank Vosburgh & Frank Lazarus
"I Met a Girl"	*Bells Are Ringing*	Jule Styne & Betty Comden & Adolph Green
"I Want To Make Magic"	*Fame*	Steve Margoshes & Jacques Levy
"I Wish I Were in Love Again"	*Babes in Arms*	Richard Rodgers & Lorenz Hart
"I'd Sure Like To Give it a Shot"	*Look To The Lilies*	Jule Styne & Sammy Cahn
"I'm Back in Circulation"	*Redhead*	Albert Hague & Dorothy Fields
"I'm Beginning To See The Light"	*Sophisticated Ladies*	Duke Ellington & Harry James
"I'm Calm"	*A Funny Thing Happened On The Way To The Forum*	Stephen Sondheim
"I'm in Love"	*The Rothschilds*	Jerry Bock & Sheldon Harnick
"Kansas City"	*Oklahoma!*	Richard Rodgers & Oscar Hammerstein
"King of The World"	*Songs For a New World*	Jason Robert Brown
"Kite, The"	*You're a Good Man, Charlie Brown*	Clark Gesner
"Lost in the Wilderness"	*Children of Eden*	Stephen Schwartz
"Me"	*Beauty and the Beast*	Alan Menken & Tim Rice
"Newsboy"	*Working*	Stephen Schwartz
"New Fangled Preacher Man"	*Purlie*	Peter Udell & Gary Geld
"Next To Lovin' I Like Fightin'"	*Shenandoah*	Peter Udell & Gary Geld
"Nothing Can Stop Me Now"	*The Roar of the Greasepaint The Smell of the Crowd*	Leslie Bricusse & Anthony Newley
"Pass The Football"	*Wonderful Town*	Leonard Bernstein & Betty Comden & Adolph Green
"Run and Tell That"	*Hairspray*	Marc Shaiman & Scott Wittman
"She Likes Basketball"	*Promises, Promises*	Burt Bacharach & Hal David
"She Loves Me"	*She Loves Me*	Jerry Bock & Sheldon Harnick
"Sitting Pretty"	*Cabaret*	John Kander & Fred Ebb
"Snoopy"	*You're a Good Man, Charlie Brown*	Clark Gesner
"They Go Wild Simply Wild Over Me"	*Irene*	Harry Carroll & Joe McCarthy & Fred Fisher
"Tonight at Eight"	*She Loves Me*	Jerry Bock & Sheldon Harnick
"Try Me"	*She Loves Me*	Jerry Bock & Sheldon Harnick
"What Am I Doing?"	*Closer Than Ever*	Richard Maltby Jr. & David Shire
"When I'm Not Near The Girl I Love"	*Finian's Rainbow*	Burton Lane & E.Y. Harburg
"Where Was I When They Passed Out Luck?"	*Minnie's Boys*	Larry Grossman & Hal Hackady
"Winter's on the Wing"	*The Secret Garden*	Lucy Simon & Marsha Norman
"Young and Healthy"	*42nd Street*	Harry Warren & Al Dubin
"You've Got That Thing"	*Fifty Million Frenchman*	Cole Porter

FEMALE UPTEMPOS

"A Little Brains – a Little Talent"	*Damn Yankees*	Richard Adler & Jerry Ross
"A Little Girl From Little Rock"	*Lorelei*	Jule Styne & Leo Robin
"Always a Bridesmaid"	*I Love You, You're Perfect, Now Change*	Joe DiPietro & Jimmy Roberts
"Always True To You in My Fashion"	*Kiss Me, Kate*	Cole Porter
"Anything Goes"	*Anything Goes*	Cole Porter
"Beguine, The"	*Dames at Sea*	Jim Wise & George Haimsohn
"Best in the World, The"	*A Day in Hollywood— A Night in the Ukraine*	Jerry Herman
"Boy Wanted"	*My One and Only*	George & Ira Gershwin
"Cockeyed Optimist"	*South Pacific*	Richard Rodgers & Oscar Hammerstein II
"Coffee in a Cardboard Cup"	*70 Girls, 70*	John Kander & Fred Ebb
"English Teacher"	*Bye Bye Birdie*	Charles Strouse & Lee Adams
"Everybody's Girl"	*Steel Pier*	John Kander & Fred Ebb
"Falling Out of Love Can Be Fun"	*Miss Liberty*	Irving Berlin
"Gentleman Is a Dope, The"	*Allegro*	Richard Rodgers & Oscar Hammerstein II
"Gimmie Gimmie"	*Thoroughly Modern Millie*	Jeanine Tesori & Dick Scanlon
"Girl in the Mirror, The"	*Grand Hotel*	Maury Yeston
"Gooch's Song"	*Mame*	Jerry Herman
"Gorgeous"	*The Apple Tree*	Jerry Bock & Sheldon Harnick
"Happily Ever After"	*Once Upon a Mattress*	Mary Rodgers & Marshall Barer
"Happy To Keep His Dinner Warm"	*How To Succeed in Business Without Really Trying*	Frank Loesser
"He Needs Me Now"	*Golden Rainbow*	Walter Marks
"He's Here"	*How Now Dow Jones*	Elmer Bernstein & Carolyn Leigh
"How Can I Wait?"	*Paint Your Wagon*	Alan Jay Lerner & Frederick Loewe
"How Lovely To Be a Woman"	*Bye Bye Birdie*	Charles Strouse & Lee Adams
"Hurry, It's Lovely Up Here"	*On a Clear Day You Can See Forever*	Burton Lane & E.Y. Harburg
"I Cain't Say No"	*Oklahoma*	Richard Rodgers & Oscar Hammerstein II
"I Can Cook Too"	*On The Town*	Leonard Bernstein & Betty Comden & Adolph Green
"I Could Have Danced All Night"	*My Fair Lady*	Alan Jay Lerner & Frederick Loewe
"I Could've Gone To Nashville"	*Nunsense*	Danny Goggin
"I Enjoy Being a Girl"	*Flower Drum Song*	Richard Rodgers & Oscar Hammerstein II
"I Got Love"	*Purlie*	Peter Udell & Gary Geld
"I Got The Sun in the Morning"	*Annie Get Your Gun*	Irving Berlin
"I Have Confidence"	*Sound of Music* (Film)	Richard Rodgers
"I Know Things Now"	*Into The Woods*	Stephen Sondheim
"I Love a Cop"	*Fiorello*	Jerry Bock & Sheldon Harnick
"I Love a Piano"	*Stop! Look! Listen!*	Irving Berlin
"I Love What I'm Doing"	*Lorelei*	Jule Styne & Leo Robin
"I Think I May Want To Remember Today"	*Starting Here, Starting Now*	Richard Maltby Jr. & David Shire
"I Want To Be Happy"	*No, No, Nanette*	Vincent Youmans & Irving Caesar
"I'll Marry The Very Next Man"	*Fiorello*	Jerry Bock & Sheldon Harnick
"I'll Show Him"	*Plain and Fancy*	Albert Hague & Arnold Horwitt
"I'm Just Wild About Harry"	*Shuffle Along*	Eubie Blake & Noble Sissle
"I'm Not Afraid of Anything"	*Songs For a New World*	Jason Robert Brown
"I'm Not at All in Love"	*The Pajama Game*	Richard Adler & Jerry Ross
"If I Were a Bell"	*Guys and Dolls*	Frank Loesser
"In My Own Little Corner"	*Cinderella*	Richard Rodgers & Oscar Hammerstein II
"It's Me"	*Me and Juliet*	Richard Rodgers & Oscar Hammerstein II
"Johnny One Note"	*Babes in Arms*	Richard Rodgers & Lorenz Hart

"Look What Happened To Mabel"	*Mack and Mabel*	Jerry Herman
"Mama Will Provide"	*Once on This Island*	Stephen Flaherty & Lynn Ahrens
"Miller's Son"	*A Little Night Music*	Stephen Sondheim
"My New Philosophy"	*You're a Good Man, Charlie Brown*	Andrew Lippa
"No Man is Worth It"	*Dance a Little Closer*	Charles Strouse & Alan Jay Lerner
"Nobody Does It Like Me"	*Seesaw*	Cy Coleman & Dorothy Fields
"Nobody Makes a Pass at Me"	*Pins and Needles*	Harold Rome
"Nothing"	*A Chorus Line*	Marvin Hamlisch & Edward Kleban
"On The Other Side of the Tracks"	*Little Me*	Cy Coleman & Carolyn Leigh
"Purlie"	*Purlie*	Peter Udell & Gary Geld
"Ragtime Romeo"	*Delilah*	John LaTouche & James Mundy
"Rhode Island is Famous For You"	*Inside USA*	Arthur Schwartz & Howard Dietz
"Shopping Around"	*Wish You Were Here*	Harold Rome
"Show Me"	*My Fair Lady*	Alan Jay Lerner & Frederick Loewe
"Shy"	*Once Upon a Mattress*	Mary Rodgers & Marshall Barer
"South America, Take It Away"	*Call Me Mister*	Harold Rome
"Spark of Creation, The"	*Children of Eden*	Stephen Schwartz
"That'll Show Him"	*A Funny Thing Happened on the Way To The Forum*	Stephen Sondheim
"There Once Was a Man"	*The Pajama Game*	Richard Adler & Jerry Ross
"Vanilla Ice Cream"	*She Loves Me*	Jerry Bock & Sheldon Harnick
"Waiting For Life"	*Once On This Island*	Stephen Flaherty & Lynn Ahrens
"What Did I Ever See in Him?"	*Bye Bye Birdie*	Charles Strouse & Lee Adams
"What Do You Think I Am?"	*Best Foot Forward*	Hugh Martin & Ralph Blane
"What's Goin' On Here?"	*Paint Your Wagon*	Alan Jay Lerner & Frederick Loewe
"Wherever He Ain't"	*Mack and Mabel*	Jerry Herman
"Without You"	*My Fair Lady*	Alan Jay Lerner & Frederick Loewe
"World Must Be Bigger Than an Avenue, The"	*Irene*	Wally Harper & Jack Lloyd
"Yes, My Heart"	*Carnival*	Bob Merrill
"You Can Always Count on Me"	*City of Angels*	Cy Coleman & David Zippel
"You Don't' Tell Me"	*No Strings*	Richard Rodgers
"You'd Better Love Me"	*High Spirits*	Hugh Martin & Ralph Blane
"You've Got Possibilities"	*It's a Bird, It's a Plane, It's Superman*	Charles Strouse & Lee Adams

FEMALE BALLADS

"A Little Bit of Love"	*Wonderful Town*	Leonard Bernstein & Betty Comden & Adolph Green
"All For You"	*Saturday Night*	Stephen Sondheim
"As Long as He Needs Me"	*Oliver!*	Lionel Bart
"Times Like This"	*Lucky Stiff*	Stephen Flaherty & Lynn Ahrens
"Before I Gaze At You"	*Camelot*	Alan Jay Lerner & Frederick Loewe
"Bewitched"	*Pal Joey*	Richard Rodgers & Lorenz Hart
"Boy Next Door, The"	*Meet Me in St. Louis*	Hugh Martin & Ralph Blane
"Buddy Beware"	*Anything Goes*	Cole Porter
"Chain of Love"	*The Grass Harp*	Claibe Richardson & Kenward Elmsie
"Change in Me, A"	*Beauty and the Beast*	Alan Menken & Time Rice
"Colors of the Wind"	*Pocahantas* (Film)	Alan Menken & Stephen Schwartz
"Come Down From The Tree"	*Once On This Island*	Stephen Flaherty & Lynn Ahrens
"Come To Your Senses"	*Tick, Tick ... BOOM!*	Jonathan Larson
"Disneyland"	*Smile*	Marvin Hamlisch & Howard Ashman
"Easy To Be Hard"	*Hair*	Galt MacDermot & James Rado & Jerome Ragni

Song	Show	Composer/Lyricist
"Embraceable You"	Crazy For You	George & Ira Gershwin
"Falling in Love With Love"	The Boys From Syracuse	Richard Rodgers & Lorenz Hart
"Far From The Home I Love"	Fiddler on the Roof	Jerry Bock & Sheldon Harnick
"Frank Mills"	Hair	Galt MacDermot & James Rado & Jerome Ragni
"Goodnight, My Someone"	The Music Man	Meredith Willson
"He Can Do It"	Purlie	Peter Udell & Gary Geld
"Hello, Young Lovers"	The King and I	Richard Rodgers & Oscar Hammerstein II
"Hold On"	The Secret Garden	Lucy Simon & Marsha Norman
"Home"	Beauty and the Beast	Alan Menken & Tim Rice
"Home"	Phantom	Maury Yeston
"Home"	The Wiz	Charlie Smalls
"How Are Things in Glocca Morra?"	Finian's Rainbow	Burton Lane & E.Y. Harburg
"How Did We Come To This?"	The Wild Party	Andrew Lippa
"How Long Has This Been Going On?"	Funny Face	George & Ira Gershwin
"I Don't Know How To Love Him"	Jesus Christ Superstar	Andrew Lloyd Webber & Tim Rice
"I Got Lost in His Arms"	Annie Get Your Gun	Irving Berlin
"I Like Him"	Drat! The Cat!	Milton Shafer & Ira Levin
"I Loved You Once in Silence"	Camelot	Alan Jay Lerner & Frederick Loewe
"I Wish I Didn't Love You So"	The Perils of Pauline (Film)	Frank Loesser
"I Wish it So"	Juno	Mark Blitzstein
"I'd Give My Life To You"	Miss Saigon	Claude-Michel Schonberg & Richard Maltby Jr. & Alain Boublil
"I'll Know"	Guys and Dolls	Frank Loesser
"I'm Always Chasing Rainbows"	Irene	Harry Carroll & Joseph McCarthy
"I'm in Love With a Soldier Boy"	Something For The Boys	Cole Porter
"I've Got a Feeling I'm Falling"	Ain't Misbehavin'	Fats Waller & Billy Rose
"I've Never Said I Love You"	Dear World	Jerry Herman
"I've Told Every Little Star"	Music in the Air	Jerome Kern & Oscar Hammerstein II
"If I Loved You"	Carousel	Richard Rodgers & Oscar Hammerstein II
"Is It Really Me?"	110 in the Shade	Harvey Schmidt & Tom Jones
"It Might As Well Be Spring"	State Fair	Richard Rodgers & Oscar Hammerstein II
"It Never Entered My Mind"	Higher and Higher	Richard Rodgers & Lorenz Hart
"It's Not Too Late"	Romance/Romance	Keith Herrmann & Barry Harman
"Jimmy"	Thoroughly Modern Millie	James Van Heusen & Sammy Cahn
"Just For Tonight"	They're Playing My Song	Marvin Hamlisch & Carole Bayer Sager
"Just Imagine"	Good News	Buddy De Sylva & Lew Brown & Ray Henderson
"Look to the Rainbow"	Finian's Rainbow	Burton Lane & E.Y. Harburg
"Lord and Master"	The King and I	Richard Rodgers & Oscar Hammerstein II
"Love, Look Away"	Flower Drum Song	Richard Rodgers & Oscar Hammerstein II
"Lovely Night, A"	Cinderella	Richard Rodgers & Oscar Hammerstein II
"Mira"	Carnival	Bob Merrill
"Moonshine Lullaby"	Annie Get Your Gun	Irving Berlin
"Mr. Snow"	Carousel	Richard Rodgers & Oscar Hammerstein II
"My Own Morning"	Hallelujah, Baby	Jule Styne & Betty Comden & Adolph Green
"My White Knight"	The Music Man	Meredith Willson
"Notice Me, Horton"	Seussical	Stephen Flaherty & Lynn Ahrens
"Once You Lose Your Heart"	Me and My Girl	Noel Gay
"One Boy"	Bye Bye Birdie	Charles Strouse & Lee Adams
"Poor Sweet Baby"	Snoopy!!!	Larry Grossman & Hal Hackady
"Quiet Thing, A"	Flora, The Red Menace	John Kander & Fred Ebb

"Raining in My Heart"	*Dames At Sea*	Jim Wise & George Haimsohn
"Simple Little Things"	*110 in the Shade*	Harvey Schmidt & Tom Jones
"Somebody, Somewhere"	*The Most Happy Fella*	Frank Loesser
"Somewhere That's Green"	*Little Shop of Horrors*	Alan Menken & Howard Ashman
"Earth and Other Minor Things, The"	*Gigi*	Alan Jay Lerner & Frederick Loewe
"There's a Fine, Fine Line"	*Avenue Q*	Jeff Marx & Robert Lopez
"They Say It's Wonderful"	*Annie Get Your Gun*	Irvin Berlin
"Till There Was You"	*The Music Man*	Meredith Willson
"Waiting For My Dearie"	*Brigadoon*	Alan Jay Lerner & Frederick Loewe
"What Did I Have That I Don't Have?"	*On a Clear Day You Can See Forever*	Burton Lane & Alan Jay Lerner
"What Makes Me Love Him?"	*The Apple Tree*	Jerry Bock & Sheldon Harnick
"What's the Use of Wonderin'?"	*Carousel*	Richard Rodgers & Oscar Hammerstein II
"When Did I Fall in Love?"	*Fiorello*	Jerry Bock & Sheldon Harnick
"Who Knows?"	*I Can Get it For You Wholesale*	Harold Rome
"Will He Like Me?"	*She Loves Me*	Jerry Bock & Sheldon Harnick
"You Ought To Be Here With Me"	*Big River*	Roger Miller

MALE BALLADS

"A Fellow Needs a Girl"	*Allegro*	Richard Rodgers & Oscar Hammerstein II
"A Man Doesn't Know"	*Damn Yankees*	Richard Adler & Jerry Ross
"All At Once You Love Her"	*Pipe Dream*	Richard Rodgers & Oscar Hammerstein II
"All Through The Night"	*Anything Goes*	Cole Porter
"Almost Like Being in Love"	*Brigadoon*	Alan Jay Lerner & Frederick Loewe
"Alone in the Universe"	*Seussical*	Stephen Flaherty & Lynn Ahrens
"Baby, Talk To Me"	*Bye Bye Birdie*	Charles Strouse & Lee Adams
"Be a Lion"	*The Wiz*	Charlie Smalls
"Come To Me, Bend To Me"	*Brigadoon*	Alan Jay Lerner & Frederick Loewe
"Different"	*Honk!*	George Stiles & Anthony Drewe
"Do I Love You Because You're Beautiful?"	*Cinderella*	Richard Rodgers & Oscar Hammerstein II
"From This Day On"	*Brigadoon*	Alan Jay Lerner & Frederick Loewe
"Girl That I Marry, The"	*Annie Get Your Gun*	Irving Berlin
"Go the Distance"	*Hercules* (Film)	Alan Menken & David Zippel
"Good Thing Going"	*Merrily We Roll Along*	Stephen Sondheim
"Goodbye Old Girl"	*Damn Yankees*	Richard Adler & Jerry Ross
"Hey, There"	*The Pajama Game*	Richard Adler & Jerry Ross
"I Believe in You"	*How To Succeed in Business Without Really Trying*	Frank Loesser
"I Chose Right"	*Baby*	Richard Maltby Jr. & David Shire
"I Could Write a Book"	*Pal Joey*	Richard Rodgers & Lorenz Hart
"I Have Dreamed"	*The King and I*	Richard Rodgers & Oscar Hammerstein II
"I Hear Bells"	*Starting Here, Starting Now*	Richard Maltby Jr. & David Shire
"I Talk To The Trees"	*Paint Your Wagon*	Alan Jay Lerner & Frederick Loewe
"I'd Rather Be Sailing"	*A New Brain*	William Finn
"I'll Never Say No"	*The Unsinkable Molly Brown*	Meredith Willson
"I've Gotta Be Me"	*Golden Rainbow*	Walter Marks
"I've Just Seen Her"	*All American*	Charles Strouse & Lee Adams
"I've Never Been in Love Before"	*Guys and Dolls*	Frank Loesser
"If Ever I Would Leave You"	*Camelot*	Alan Jay Lerner & Frederick Loewe
"If I Can't Love Her"	*Beauty and the Beast*	Alan Menken & Tim Rice
"If I Loved You"	*Carousel*	Richard Rodgers & Oscar Hammerstein II
"If I Rule The World"	*Pickwick*	Leslie Bricusse & Cyril Ornadel

"It Only Takes a Moment"	*Hello, Dolly!*	Jerry Herman
"It's Hard To Speak My Heart"	*Parade*	Jason Robert Brown
"It's You"	*Dames At Sea*	Jim Wise & George Haimsohn
"Johanna"	*Sweeney Todd*	Stephen Sondheim
"Leavin's Not The Only Way To Go"	*Big River*	Roger Miller
"Lonely House"	*Street Scene*	Kurt Weil & Langston Hughes
"Lonely Room"	*Oklahoma!*	Richard Rodgers & Oscar Hammerstein II
"Lonely Town"	*On the Town*	Leonard Bernstein & Betty Comden & Adolph Green
"Love, I Hear"	*A Funny Thing Happened On The Way To The Forum*	Stephen Sondheim
"Lucky To Be Me"	*On The Town*	Leonard Bernstein & Betty Comden & Adolph Green
"Mama, A Rainbow"	*Minnie's Boys*	Larry Grossman & Hal Hackady
"Marry Me"	*Rink, The*	John Kander & Fred Ebb
"Mason, The"	*Working*	Craig Carnelia
"My Romance"	*Jumbo*	Richard Rodgers & Lorenz Hart
"New Town is a Blue Town, A"	*The Pajama Game*	Richard Adler & Jerry Ross
"Nine O'Clock"	*Take Me Along*	Bob Merrill
"Not While I'm Around"	*Sweeney Todd*	Stephen Sondheim
"Now I Have Everything"	*Fiddler on The Roof*	Jerry Bock & Sheldon Harnick
"On The Street Where You Live"	*My Fair Lady*	Alan Jay Lerner & Frederick Loewe
"Only Home I Know, The"	*Shenandoah*	Peter Udell & Gary Geld
"Pretty Girl is Like a Melody, A"	*Ziegfeld Follies of 1919*	Irving Berlin
"Proud of Your Boy"	*Hercules*	Alan Menken & Howard Ashman
"Real Live Girl"	*Little Me*	Cy Coleman & Carolyn Leigh
"River in the Rain"	*Big River*	Roger Miller
"Rosie"	*Bye Bye Birdie*	Charles Strouse & Lee Adams
"Santa Fe"	*Newsies* (Film)	Alan Menken & Jack Feldman
"She Touched Me"	*Drat! The Cat!*	Milton Shafer & Ira Levin
"Sidewalk Tree"	*Raisin*	Robert Brittan & Judd Wolden
"Some Girls"	*Once on This Island*	Stephen Flaherty & Lynn Ahrens
"Tell My Father"	*Civil War*	Frank Wildhorn & Jack Murphy
"Ten Minutes Ago"	*Cinderella*	Richard Rodgers & Oscar Hammerstein II
"There Go For You But I"	*Brigadoon*	Alan Jay Lerner & Frederick Loewe
"There's a Room in My House"	*A Family Affair*	John Kander & John Goldman
"There's a Small Hotel"	On Your Toes	Richard Rodgers & Lorenz Hart
"There's Something About You"	*Dames At Sea*	Jim Wise & George Haimsohn
"They Didn't Believe Me"	*Girl From Utah, The*	Jerome Kern & Herbert Reynolds
"Too Much in Love To Care"	*Sunset Boulevard*	Andrew Lloyd Webber & Don Black
"Try To Remember"	*Fantasticks, The*	Harvey Schmidt & Tom Jones
"Wait Till You See Her"	*By Jupiter*	Richard Rodgers & Lorenz Hart
"Waiting For The Light To Shine"	*Big River*	Roger Miller
"Want To Go Home, I"	*Big*	Richard Maltby Jr. & David Shire
"Where or When?"	*Babes in Arms*	Richard Rodgers & Lorenz Hart
"With You"	*Baby*	Richard Maltby Jr. & David Shire
"With You"	*Pippin*	Stephen Schwartz
"With You On My Arm"	*La Cage Aux Folles*	Jerry Herman
"You are Beautiful"	*Flower Drum Song*	Richard Rodgers & Oscar Hammerstein II
"You've Come Home"	*Wildcat*	Cy Coleman & Carolyn Leigh
"Younger Than Springtime"	*South Pacific*	Richard Rodgers & Oscar Hammerstein II

Audition Material Portfolio

16 Bars Audition

Up-tempo _____

Ballad _____

Broadway Show Tunes

1900–1920 Up-tempo _____

1900–1920 Ballad _____

1920s–1930s Up-tempo _____

1920s–1930s Ballad _____

1940s Up-tempo _____

1940s Ballad _____

1950s Up-tempo _____

1950s Ballad _____

1960s–Present Up-tempo _____

1960s–Present Ballad _____

Special Material

Comedy Song _____

Patter Song _____

Song & Dance _____

Country/Folk _____

Contemporary Pop/Rock _____

Gospel/R&B _____

Story Song _____

Legit/Operetta _____

Jazz/Swing _____

1950s Rock 'n' Roll _____

1960s Rock 'n' Roll _____

Permissions

Fences by August Wilson, Copyright ©1986 by August Wilson. Used by permission of Dutton Signet, a division of Penguin Group (USA) Inc.

The Shadow Box by Michael Cristofer, Copyright ©1977 by Michael Cristofer. Caution: Professionals and amateurs are hereby warned that *The Shadow Box*, being fully protected under the copyright laws of the United States of America, the British Commonwealth countries, including Canada, and the other countries of the Copyright Union, is subject to a royalty. All rights, including professional, amateur, motion picture, recitation, public reading, radio, television and cable broadcasting, and the rights of translation into foreign languages, are strictly reserved. Any inquiry regarding the availability of performance rights, or the purchase of individual copies of the authorized acting edition, must be directed to Samuel French Inc., 45 West 25th Street, New York, NY 10010, with other locations in Hollywood and Toronto, Canada.

Blithe Spirit by Noel Coward. Methuen Publishing Limited. Copyright © The Estate of Noel Coward.

Buried Child by Sam Shepard. Copyright ©1979 by Sam Shepard. Copyright ©1981 Random House Inc.

Greensboro (A Requiem). Copyright ©1996 by Emily Mann. From *Testimonies: Four Plays by Emily Mann* ©1997. Theatre Communication Group, 520 Eighth Avenue, New York, NY 10018-4156.

Jack And Jill. Caution: Professionals and amateurs are hereby warned that *Jack and Jill* ©1995, 1996 by Alexander Speer, Trustee, is subject to a royalty. It is fully protected under the copyright laws of the United States of America, the British Commonwealth, including Canada, and all other countries of the Copyright Union. All rights, including professional, amateur, motion picture, recitation, lecturing, public reading, radio broadcasting, television, and the rights of translation into foreign languages are strictly reserved. In its present form, the play is dedicated to the reading public only. The amateur live stage performance rights to the play are controlled exclusively by Samuel French, Inc., and royalty arrangements and licenses must be secured well in advance of presentation. Royalty of the required amount must be paid whether the play is presented for charity or gain and whether or not admission is charged. No part of this work may be reproduced, stored in a retrieval system or transmitted in any form, by any means, now known or yet to be invented, including mechanical, electronic, photocopying, recording, video-taping or otherwise, without the prior written permission of the Trustee. Particular emphasis is laid on the question of amateur or professional readings, permission, and terms for which must be secured in writing from Samuel French, Inc., 45 West 25th Street, New York, NY 10010.

Promenade. Reprinted by permission of Helen Merrill Ltd. on behalf of the Author. Copyright ©1987 by Maria Irene Fornes.

The Danube. Reprinted by permission of Helen Merrill Ltd. on behalf of the Author. Copyright ©1981 by Maria Irene Fornes.

Free Gift. Copyright ©1996, 2004 by Fountain Pen, Inc. Reprinted by permission of William Morris Agency, Inc. on behalf of the Author by special arrangement with Samuel French, Inc. All rights reserved. *Free Gift* was originally produced by Gloucester Stage, Gloucester, MA in 1996. *Free Gift* was published in *Israel Horovitz: Collected Works, Volume III—The Primary English Class and Six New Plays*, published in 1996 by Smith and Kraus. Caution: Professionals and amateurs are hereby warned that *Free Gift* is subject to a royalty. It is fully protected under the copyright laws of the United States of America and of all countries covered by the International Copyright Union (including the Dominion of Canada and the rest of the British Commonwealth), the Berne Convention, the Pan-American Copyright Convention, and the Universal Copyright Convention as well as all countries with which the United States has reciprocal copyright relations. All rights, including professional/amateur stage rights, motion picture, recitation, lecturing, public reading, radio broadcasting, television, video or sound recording, all other forms of mechanical or electronic reproduction, such as CD-ROM, CD-I, information storage and retrieval systems and photocopying, and the rights of translation into foreign languages, are strictly reserved. Particular emphasis is laid upon the matter of readings, permission for which must be secured from the author's agent in writing. Inquiries concerning rights should be addressed to: William Morris Agency, Inc., 1325 Avenue of the Americas, New York, NY 10019, Attn: Jack Tantleff.

Sunshine. Copyright ©1989 by William Mastrosimone. Reprinted by permission of William Morris Agency, Inc. on behalf of the Author. *Sunshine* was originally produced in 1989 by the Circle Repertory Company, New York City. All rights reserved. Caution: Professionals and amateurs are hereby warned that *Sunshine* is subject to a royalty. It is fully protected under the copyright laws of the United States of America and of all countries covered by the International Copyright Union (including the Dominion of Canada and the rest of the British Commonwealth), the Berne Convention, the Pan-American Copyright Convention, and the Universal Copyright Convention as well as all countries with which the United states has reciprocal copyright relations. All rights, including professional/amateur stage rights, motion picture, recitation, lecturing, public reading, radio broadcasting, television, video or sound recording, all other forms of mechanical or electronic reproduction, such as CD-ROM, CD-I, information storage and retrieval systems and photocopying, and the rights of translation into foreign languages, are strictly reserved. Particular emphasis is laid upon the matter of readings, permission for which must be secured from the author's agent in writing. Inquiries concerning rights should be addressed to: William Morris Agency, Inc, 1325 Avenue of the Americas, New York, NY 10019.

The Rainmaker. Copyright ©1955 by N. Richard Nash. Reprinted by permission of William Morris Agency, Inc. on behalf of the Author.

The Man I Love, by George and Ira Gershwin. Copyright ©1924 (Renewed), WB Music Corp. (ASCAP). All rights reserved. Warner Brothers Publications U.S., Inc., Miami, FL 33014.

Index

About the Authors

DARREN R. COHEN is a conductor, musical director, vocal coach, and pianist working at theaters around the country and in New York City. He has collaborated with some of the top names in musical theater, such as Stephen Sondheim, Jerry Herman, Donna McKechnie, Jule Styne, Karen Ziemba, Richard Alder, Malcolm Gets, Anita Gillette, Roslyn Kind, Rue McClanahan, Marni Nixon, Sally Ann Howes, Georgia Engel, Dean Pitchford, and John Kander, to name a few. His Broadway credits range from *A Chorus Line* to *Chicago*. Also in New York, Darren was the musical director of *Zombie Prom* (at Variety Arts Theatre), *Carnival* (for The York Theatre Company; Outer Critics Circle Award for Best Revival), *A . . . My Name Is Still Alice* (at Second Stage Theatre), *The Fantasticks* (at Sullivan Street Playhouse), *Show Me Where the Good Times Are* (for Jewish Repertory Theatre), and *Anyone Can Whistle* (at Forty-Seventh Street Theatre). He also played keyboards for *And The World Goes 'Round* (at West Side Arts).

Darren's regional credits include *Side by Side by Sondheim* (Coconut Grove Playhouse) *Footloose* (Sacramento Music Circus), *Cabaret and Follies* (Barrington Stage Company, Great Barrington, Massachusetts), *A Grand Night for Singing* and *Zorba* (North Shore Music Theatre), *The Hot Mikado* (San Jose CLO), *Little Shop of Horrors* (MUNY/Kansas City Starlight), *Make Someone Happy* (Theater on the Square, San Francisco), *Assassins* (Players Theater, Columbus, Ohio), *Flora, the Red Menace* and *Closer Than Ever* (Westport Playhouse), *Jacques Brel Is Alive and Well and Living in Paris* and *A Little Night Music* (Cincinnati Playhouse), and *Beehive* (Asolo Theatre Company).

Among Darren's national tours have been *Chicago, Entirely Sophie, Grease, Some Enchanted Evening, Hey Ma . . . Kaye Ballard,* and *Donna McKechnie . . . Inside the Music.* Recordings include the original cast album of *Zombie Prom* and *Ben Bagley's Broadway Revisited.* Based in New York City, Darren is on the faculty at New York University and is a graduate of the prestigious Eastman School of Music.

MICHAEL PERILSTEIN has been a professional actor since the age of eight, working in the industry for over twenty-five years. He has worked in television and film, and on Broadway, Off-Broadway, and on the radio. A member of the performers unions AFTRA, EQUITY, and SAG, Michael holds a Master of Fine Arts in Performance from the University of Virginia. He is the cofounder and President of Walleyed Productions, Inc., a nonprofit New York City theater company that produces and performs new works for the stage.

Michael has taught acting workshops to hundreds of students and actors over the years. His teaching credits include: Columbia University, Hofstra University, New York University, Skidmore College, and the University of Virginia. Currently, he teaches acting, improvisation, and monologue workshops at the American Musical and Dramatic Academy (AMDA) in Manhattan. Michael was born, raised, and lives in New Jersey.

Visit www.completeprofessionalaudition.com.

Copyright © 2005 by Darren R. Cohen and Michael Perilstein
Illustrations © 2005 by Chad Thompson

First published in the United States in 2005 by Back Stage Books
an imprint of Watson-Guptill Publications
a division of VNU Business Media, Inc.
770 Broadway, New York, New York 10003
www.watsonguptill.com

Senior Editor: Mark Glubke
Editors: Michèle LaRue, Meryl Greenblatt
Cover Design: John Clifford/Platinum Design
Design: Cheryl Viker
Production Manager: Ellen Greene
Library of Congress Control Number: 2005923699

All rights reserved. No part of this publication may be reproduced or used in any form or
by any means—graphic, electronic, or mechanical, including photocopying, recording, taping,
or information storage-and-retrieval systems—without the prior permission of the Publisher.

ISBN: 0-8230-7683-0
Printed in the United States of America
First printing, 2005
1 2 3 4 5 6 7 8 9/13 12 11 10 09 08 07 06 05

The Complete Professional Audition

A Commonsense Guide to Auditioning for Musicals and Plays

DARREN R. COHEN WITH MICHAEL PERILSTEIN

With illustrations by Chad Thompson

BACK STAGE BOOKS
an imprint of Watson-Guptill Publications
New York